D1476017

AHADITH
FOR
CHILDREN

ABDUL RAUF

EDITED AND REVISED BY

LALEH BAKHTIAR

Library of Islam

Book designer

Liaquat Ali

Library of Congress Cataloging in Publication Data

Rauf, A.
    Ahadith for Children.
    1. Islam. 2. Hadith. 3. Juvenile Literature.
    ISBN: 0-933511-14-0

Published by the Library of Islam
P. O. Box 595
South Elgin IL 60177

Distributed by
KAZI Publications, Inc.
3023 W. Belmont Avenue
Chicago IL 60618
Tel: 312-267-7001; FAX: 312-267-7002

To Prophet Muhammad (ﷺ)
who was sent by God as a *"Mercy
for humanity"* (21:107)

CONTENTS

Preface to the First Edition

It is indeed a pleasant privilege for me to present *Ahadith for Children*. During the preparation of this book I had the honor to consult a number of standard books on Traditions (*ahadith*)—the sayings of the Prophet (ﷺ). In addition, I was constantly guided by several specialists on the subject. I owe them all a deep sense of gratitude.

The basic purpose of this book, the first of its kind in the world, is too obvious. An attempt has been to project the simple and easy-to-understand Traditions of the Prophet that pertain to children's everyday life. The idea is to provide the modern child a useful source of reliable guidance. Prophet Muhammad's guidance has already been found to possess magic powers of transforming human character and personality.

There could be no better earthly food for children's thought nor a better direction for their behavior than the wholesome guidance from the greatest benefactor of humanity. The Prophet made history in the realm of affection for children and the development of their personality and character.

Ahadith for Children, however, is not meant for children alone. Anybody, young or old, living anywhere in the world, who may be desirous of remodeling his or her thought and behavior on reliable foundations, could confidently feel that this multi purpose book was meant for his or her knowledge and his or her guidance as well.

A.R.
1976

Preface to the Tenth Revised Edition

The Library of Islam is happy to offer the tenth edition of this work to you. There have been extensive changes in the format while the content remains the same. The format is now that of a textbook with questions and answers for each section. The questions take the form of Identification, Clarification or Discussion. While the companion book to this, *Quran for Children*, emphasized Identification and Clarification, this work, *Ahadith for Children*, emphasizes Discussion between the teacher and students. Discussion furthers cognitive development in the children and helps them formulate questions they themselves may have. Therefore, it is considered to be a higher form of cognitive development.

For instance one Tradition of the Prophet (ﷺ) says that we should take a bath one day a week. For children growing up in the West, this may seem not to be often enough. Listening to the news, they also hear how people in other parts of the world face a scarity of water. As Islam is a universal religion which has solutions for all people, for the Prophet (☺) to have recommended a daily bath would be to recommend something which is not possible for all people of the world. Through discussion with the class, children realize the blessings that they have and gain sympathy for people who are less fortunate than they are.

LB
1995

1
Introduction

Section 1: Confronting the Dangers to Modern Childhood

The modern child lives in a troubled world. It is becoming increasingly charged with risks and dangers. Whether at home, on the street or at school, a variety of hazards appear to be chasing children. Of these childhood dangers. the moral hazards are assuming deadlier forms day by day. The moral situation is deteriorating further with the spread of such immoral influences as: unhealthy movies, undesirable radio and rubbish television programs, obscene literature, purposeless school activities, low company, etc. Consequently, the chances of slips and stagnation, frustration and delinquency are fast increasing for the contemporary child.

Parents and teachers all over the world are more worried than ever before about children. The more sensitive children often feel that they have been trapped in the wilderness. Being forced to live in dull, dark and dirty surroundings, many children feel depressed and even suffocated. At the same time there are a number of children who feel confused and lost. They do not realize what is happening to them and around them.

What should you as child, parent or teacher do in such an unfavorable atmosphere? Should you allow yourself to be swept away by the evil tide? Surely that would be unwise and unbecoming of a good Muslim. Should you remain disheartened and give up all hope? That would make the matter worse. What should then be done?

Certainly, the best line of action would be to face the situation with courage and confidence. Make an all-out effort to understand, to stabilize, to improve and to move forward. You would then discover that the despair and darkness change fast into hope and light. You will find that you are getting a new stamina and a new power to face the problems and perplexities of modern life. Such a brave and beneficial line of action is quite possible as well as easy. Any child anywhere in the world could do it only if he or she cares to study the Traditions of Prophet Muhammad (ﷺ).

Section 2: Moving Words and Deeds

Presented in this book is a selection of *ahadith* for the guidance of the children of the modern age. *Ahadith* (singular, *hadith*) is an Arabic word. Literally it means: "saying," "Tradition," "news," "statement," "information," "report," "communication," etc. Of these the choice of the English word "Traditions" (singular, Tradition), as an English equivalent to the Arabic word *"ahadith,"* has become extremely popular. Understood in its technical sense the word stands for the record of both the wise sayings as well as the noble doings of Prophet Muhammad (ﷺ). His words and deeds

Understood in its technical sense the word stands for the record of both the wise sayings as well as the noble doings of Prophet Muhammad (﷽). His words and deeds had a magic impact on the thought and behavior of all humanity.

Section 3: Advantages of Studying the Prophet's Traditions

The main advantages of studying the Traditions are that they are the best model for living a civilized life. They offer new hope, new power and they help us learn one of the modern world's important languages.

The Best Model of a Civilized Life

The Quran is the best possible code of guidance for all humanity. In order to develop children's interest in the Book, *Quran for Children* has already been presented. But the Traditions of the Prophet also play an extremely constructive role in developing the human personality and character. It is through these very Traditions that we are able to understand the meaning of the Quran and the purpose of life. Moreover, the Quran declares Prophet Muhammad (﷽) as the best model for all humanity. His life provides a valuable source of inspiration and a reliable guidance for every one. How did he think in happy and sad situations? What was his style of facing life and its challenges? What methods did he use to turn the worst people into the best citizens? Answers to all these significant queries are available in the Traditions of the Prophet.

Hence why not avail of this life-saving wisdom? Why not allow the magic of his words and deeds make a constructive impact on your personality and character? Whether you belong to the East or to the West you have a right to enjoy the freshness of Prophet Muhammad's developmental message. Just give a trial to this creative model of thinking and acting. You will then feel the difference yourself. You will find that you are well set on the road to peace and progress. The filth around you will then cease to cause you any damage.

New Hope, New Power

There is another charming feature of these Traditions. They are not in the form of dull and dry commandments. They are an entirely different and an inspiring system of guidance. The Prophet's words and deeds are full of peace and prosperity, light and life. They endeavor to demonstrate the difference between the right and the wrong ways of life in a forceful, interesting and practical manner. The Prophet shows humanity that the right path is definitely beneficial as well as pleasant to follow. His Traditions analyze human life and its problems very realistically. The reader himself begins to feel a strong inward urge to think and to act constructively. He or she begins to understand the difference between what is right and wrong models and feels fully prepared to follow the good and the right with full confidence. He or she feels as if he or she was armed with unusual powers to overcome all sorts of evil and ignorance.

It has been observed all over the world that the life of those children who pay heed to the Prophet's Traditions are able to effect change within themselves. The change begins to beautify their thinking, their speech, their writing and all other by the passing temptations. In fact, failure and frustration flee from their surroundings.

Modern World's Important Language

Arabic is an important world language. It is spoken in the present world's most strategic sectors. Besides, it is the language of the Quran. For a Muslim its study is all too obvious. The study of Arabic is extremely interesting and advantageous for a non-Muslim as well. It helps him or her understand the past and the present of the Muslims. Familiarity with the Arabic language helps in knowing a lot about Muslim countries of the modern world.

Is Arabic a difficult language? Not at all! How to learn it? One of the easiest ways of acquiring a working proficiency in Arabic would be to study the Traditions of the Prophet. Like the Quran the language of the *ahadith* is the simplest possible Arabic. Learning the Traditions and through it the Arabic language is thus easy as well as beneficial.

So apart from providing an ideal source for the development of personality and character, this small book serves a great cultural purpose as well. It offers an excellent opportunity to acquire a working familiarity with Arabic and the Arabic speaking people of the modern age. As a matter of fact reading the same material simultaneously in two modern languages develops efficiency in both the languages.

Section 4: Purpose of *Ahadith for Children*

Ahadith for Children is thus designed to be a multi purpose book. Its two major objectives, however, stand out far more clearly:

- Introduction to the true form and spirit of the Prophet's system of guidance
- Presentation of a most suitable and constructive reading material for children

The True Form and Spirit

The original Arabic texts of the Prophet's Traditions have been offered along with their English translations. The book, therefore, makes a successful attempt at familiarizing children with the true form and spirit, the real plan and purpose of the electrifying words and the inspiring deeds of the Prophet (ﷺ).

Constructive Material

The selection is exclusively confined to such Traditions as revolve round the modern children's life and their everyday problems. The book, then, contains constructive reading material especially meant for children. It is specially designed to provide them strong incentives to think, to reform and to develop into civilized men and women of tomorrow.

This book has been prepared mainly for children. This factor has determined the range of selection of the original *hadith* material, the choice of words in the English translation and even the mode of presentation in all the chapters. An all-out effort has been made to present easy reading material. In short, it is designed to serve as a convincing and a forceful motivator for all children of the world.

But let there be no misunderstanding. *Ahadith for Children* is not meant for children alone. There may be many grown ups, either brothers, sisters and even parents, teachers and other adults, who may have missed the earlier opportunity of studying *ahadith*. All such adults could also enjoy the beauties of the Prophet's sayings and doings. They could as well avail of their wisdom in their everyday dealings. Furthermore, such an adult use of this book will also eventually benefit the children either directly or indirectly.

Section 5: Plan of *Ahadith for Children*

The following guiding principles in selecting the Traditions have been:

• The appropriateness of the selected Tradition to the level of understanding.
• Selection of the trustworthy Traditions out of the standard books on the subject

The original source has been cited at the end of each Tradition. Side by side with the original Arabic text, easy-to-understand English translation of each Tradition has also been rendered. The language and the meaning of the selected Traditions are so simple and so convincing that any further interpretations, in addition to their faithful translation, are neither needed nor offered.

This book deals with a very important subject. It follows a definite plan. Each chapter focuses on an important aspect of life. It is further divided into smaller sections. Each section touches certain vital needs of daily life. Each issue has been illustrated exclusively in the light of the Prophet's Traditions. It is quite obvious that a working familiarity with these important matters is indispensable for the smooth and purposeful growth of a modern child's personality and character.

This small book is divided into fourteen chapters. This one is the first, introductory chapter. In order to familiarize children with the meaning, purpose and history of the Traditions and its practical role in modern life, Chapter 2 is devoted to an historical introduction. The next chapter offers a selection of such simple Traditions that throw light on the Islamic way of life. The decorum and decency of everyday life is the subject-matter of Chapter 4. The next chapter focuses on some Traditions bearing on the necessity and utility of acquiring knowledge and wisdom. This is followed by a chapter on the significance of health and hygiene. Chapter 7 is devoted to table manners and the role of hospitality.

What is a decent and graceful dress? How should a good child look? Chapter 8 discusses this important theme In the light of Prophet's Traditions. The next chapter highlights the role of good character and conduct. Respect and service of the parents is the substance of Chapter 10. What is a healthy attitude towards brothers, sisters, relatives, friends and neighbors? The Prophet's answer is available In the next chapter. Chapter 12 explains the Islamic ideas of brotherhood and mutual affection. Lying, backbiting and other varieties of offensive use of the tongue are the themes of Chapter 13. The last chapter offers some selected Traditions explaining the common aspects of bad character and unhealthy conduct. Practical hints to avoid the wrong path have also been offered.

Let's find out what you have learned from

Chapter 1: Introduction

Discussion:

1. What are the dangers to modern childhood that the author suggests? Can you think of any others?
2. What does the Arabic word *ahadith* mean in English?
3. What three suggestions does the author give as advantages to studying the Prophet's Traditions?
4. What are the author's two main objectives?
5. Discuss the plan the author uses in writing this textbook.

Section Answers:

Chapter 1: Introduction

1. Answers vary.
2. "Saying," "Tradition," "news," "statement," "information," "report," and "communication."
3. The Traditions are the best model from which we learn to live a civilized life. They give new hope, new power to us and help us learn one of the modern world's important languages.
4. Introduction to the form and spirit of the Prophet's system of guidance and presentation of a most suitable and constructive reading material for children.
5. Answers vary.

2
A Brief History of Ahadith

Section 1: Fountain of Wisdom and Guidance

Prophet Muhammad (ﷺ) was born in 571 AD in Makkah, the renowned city of Arabia. He migrated to Madinah, another famed town of the same country, in 622 CE/1 AH where he died in 632 AD. God Almighty conferred prophethood on him when he was forty. The period of prophethood lasted twenty-three years. It began in 610 CE/13 BH (before the migration to Madinah) and ended in 632 CE/11 AH, the year of his death. Hijri (H) dates are based on the lunar calendar while the common era (CE) dates are based on the solar calendar.

The last twenty-three years of his life, i.e. from 13 BH to 11 AH, are counted as a glorious era in the history of humanity. During these memorable years, Prophet Muhammad (ﷺ) continued to spread Islam, the religion of peace and progress. He uttered a large number of moving words for the guidance of humanity. He also performed a variety of pious deeds. Those words of advice and deeds of righteousness stand out as a fountain of practical wisdom and constructive guidance for all of humanity. *Ahadith*, the recorded versions of his wise words and noble deeds, is a stimulating study for all of humanity. A child, eager to forge ahead in life, must familiarize himself or herself with the essence and purpose of the Traditions.

Let's find out what you have learned from

Section 1: Fountain of Wisdom and Guidance

Identification:
1. In what year of the common era (CE) did revelation occur? And in what hijri (BH/AH) year?

Clarification:
2. The collection of the *ahadith* relate to what period of history?

Section 2: Muhammad (ﷺ) Inspires All of Humanity

Whenever Prophet Muhammad (ﷺ) uttered a word of guidance, his Companions (*ashab*) hastened to commit the same to memory. Those who knew the art of writing used to write it down. Wherever these good-natured people went, they talked about those wise sayings for the benefit of others. The Prophet's wisdom thus kept on spreading far and wide. It went on reforming humanity's thought and behavior.

After the death of the Prophet, his Companions and Successors (*tabyun*) continued the sacred mission of people's education and guidance. They carried the torch of wisdom and righteousness to adjoining lands. Wherever they went, they enlightened people on the Islamic way of life. This new way of life has been outlined in the Quran. It was actually practiced by the Prophet.

The most remarkable point was reached when the Muslims entered Spain. There they established schools, colleges, universities and libraries. Their cultural pursuits and social activities provided nourishing food for thought to all of Europe. The Islamic way of life began to be understood in the West as well. More and more people began to appreciate the meaning and purpose of the Prophet's revolutionary message. It began to bring about a constructive change in all sectors of their life. A time soon came when the Islamic way of life became popular with the people of East as well as of the West. The present day world owes much of its beauty and betterment to the noble teachings of Prophet Muhammad (ﷺ) and the humanitarian services of his followers.

Let's find out what you have learned from

Section 2: Muhammad (ﷺ) Inspires All of Humanity

Identification:

1. What is the English and Arabic word for those who wrote down or committed to memory what the Prophet (ﷺ) said and did?
2. What is the English and Arabic word for the second generation or Successors, those who wrote down what the Companions told them the Prophet (ﷺ) did or said?

Clarification:

3. Who is the perfect model of the Quran in practice?

Section 3: Main Varieties of Traditions and the Earliest Collections

Ahadith is a comprehensive word. It stands for the creative teaching and the revolutionary activities of Prophet Muhammad (☆). The major types of *ahadith* are:

(1) the narration of all those words that the Prophet uttered from time to time;

(2) the collection of specific instructions and advice which he offered for the guidance of humanity;

(3) the statements of all the deeds that he performed in the presence of his Companions;

(4) other details of his personal life as witnessed and reported by the members of his family.

The work of collecting the Prophet's sayings and recording the same systematically began while the Prophet was alive. Some of his Companions had prepared *ahadith* collections of varying sizes. Of these early collections the one prepared by Abd Allah ibn Amr ibn al-Aas (و) is very famous. This collection is known *al-Sadiq*. It contains 1000 sayings of the Prophet.

There are other collections besides the one mentioned above which were also prepared during the Prophet's lifetime. They were compiled by illustrious Companions like Abu Bakr (و), Ali (☆), Anas, Abd Allah ibn Masud, Abu Hurayra and Saad ibn Abbad (و).

Let's find out what you have learned from

Section 3: Main Varieties of Traditions and the Earliest Collections

Identification:

1. The name of the famous collection of Traditions of Abd Allah ibn Amr ibn al-Aas is?

Clarification:

2. Define the four major types of Traditions (*ahadith*).

Section 4: Developments During the Early Caliphate

After the death of Prophet Muhammad the great caliphs kept on popularizing his teachings among the people. The four early caliphs, who are specially known for this valuable service to humanity are: (1) Abu Bakr al-Siddiq (ؓ), (2) Umar al-Faruq (ؓ), (3) Uthman al-Affan (ؓ) and (4) Ali ibn Abi Talib (ؓ). These eminent statesmen are also known as the rightly-guided caliphs. Their period is referred to as the age of early caliphate.

A number of *ahadith* collections were prepared during the days of the early caliphs. Of these the one compiled by Abu Bakr al-Siddiq (ؓ) is very well known. It contains 500 Traditions. In addition, Imam Hasan (ؓ), Abu Musa Ashari and Abd Allah ibn Abbas (ؓ) also compiled different *ahadith* collections at different times.

With the end of the early caliphate began the era of the Umayyids. Umar ibn Abd al- Aziz was the eighth Umayyid caliph. It was during his rule that the task of collecting all the Traditions in one place and publishing them in the shape of a comprehensive book began on a large scale. His rule began in 717 CE/99 AH and ended in 719 CE/101 AH. During this period the Muslim empire expanded enormously. It included countries like Spain, Algeria. Morocco, Tunis, Egypt, Syria, Palestine, Iraq, Saudi Arabia, Yemen, Kuwait, Bahrain, Jordan, Asia Minor, Iran, Afghanistan and even northwestern parts of India. *Ahadith* literature was in great demand in all these areas. Caliph Umar ibn Abdul Aziz felt that there was a danger of the loss of a number of Traditions if these were not recorded in writing. He, therefore, issued immediate instructions to all of his governors and scholars that all available Traditions be recorded carefully. They were also ordered to send the same to the caliph at Damascus, which was the capital of the Umayyid empire at that time.

The enthusiasm, precaution and orderliness which the caliph displayed in undertaking this important task is unparalleled. In one of his royal decrees he ordered: Whatever Tradition of the Prophet (ﷺ) you may come across must be recorded after proper scrutiny, as I fear the loss of knowledge and the death of the scholars. But beware! Never accept any saying other than that of the Prophet nor record the same.

Damascus was soon flooded with large collections of the Prophet's Traditions. The caliph put them all in writing after further scrutiny. In this manner the different *ahadith* collections were brought together in one place for the first time in Islamic history. This all-inclusive collection then became a standard source of guidance and reference. The caliph received several copies of the same prepared under his personal supervision. One copy was placed in the central mosque of each main city of the vast empire. Consequently the recorded accounts of the sayings and the deeds of Prophet Muhammad (ﷺ) came within easy reach of everyone.

Let's find out what you have learned from

Section 4: Developments During the Early Caliphate
Identification:
1. Name the rightly-guided caliphs.
2. Name the famous 8th century caliph who ordered the Traditions be collected.

Section 5: Imam Malik's Decorated Flower Vase

The person after Caliph Umar ibn Abd al-Aziz who enjoys the reputation of systematic collection of the Prophet's Traditions and their mass circulation, is Abu Abd Allah Malik ibn Anas (ر). He is known as Imam Malik. He was a great scholar. Born in Madinah in 718CE/94 AH, he died in 795 CE/179 AH at the age of eighty-six.

Imam Malik lectured on *ahadith* for sixty-two years. His famous book on the subject is known as *Muwatta*, which means "the decorated." This great book presents the Prophet's Traditions in a tastefully decorated and carefully-arranged manner. Indeed, the style and the presentation are so charming that the book really looks like a decorated flower vase. The Imam started compiling *Muwatta* when he was thirty-seven. It was completed ten years later. The *Muwatta* includes 1,720 Traditions. It is the first highly organized collection of Traditions. The book is widely valued all over the world.

Let's find out what you have learned from

Section 5: Imam Malik's Decorated Flower Vase

Identification:

1. What is the name of Imam Malik's famous work on the Traditions?
2. What does that word mean?

Section 6: The *Musnad* of Imam Hanbal

After the *Muwatta* several other collections were produced by eminent scholars. Among these later publications *Musnad* enjoys the largest reputation. It was prepared by Imam Ahmad ibn Hanbal. He is also known as Imam Hanbal. The book contains 30,000 Traditions.

Imam Hanbal was born in 780 CE/164 AH in Baghdad, the famed capital of Iraq. He died in the same town in 835 CE/241 AH. Imam Hanbal was unusually intelligent, thoroughly pious and a reputed scholar.

Let's find out what you have learned from

Section 6: The Musnad of Imam Hanbal

Identification:

1. What is the name of Imam Hanbal's work on the Traditions?

Section 7: The Six Sound Books

After the publication of *Muwatta* and *Musnad,* a number of other *ahadith* collections also appeared at different times. The six collections which gained unusual fame are known as *siha sitta,* which means "the six sound books." These collections are: (1) *Sahih Bukhari*, (2) *Sahih Muslim*, (3) *Jami Tirmidi*, (4) *Sunan Abu Daud*, (5) *Sunan Nisai*, and (6) *Sunan lbn Majah*.

Sahih Bukhari: The compiler of this famous collection is the eminent scholar, Imam Muhammad ibn Ismail ibn Ibrahim ibn Muizz. He is popularly known as Imam Bukhari. He was born in 810 CE/194 AH in Bukhara, a famed city of Iran. He died in 870 CE/256 AH at the age of sixty-two.

Imam Bukhari worked on the book continuously for sixteen years. He finally selected 7,275 Traditions for inclusion in his collection. *Sahih Bukhari* has always been considered as the most trustworthy book on the Traditions.

Sahih Muslim: Next to *Sahih Bukhari* the authoritative book on the Traditions or *ahadith* is *Sahih Muslim.* Its compiler is Imam Muslim ibn Hallaj al-Qushari al-Nishapuri. He is also known as Imam Muslim. He was born round about 819 CE/204 AH in Nishapur, a famous town in Iran. He died in 874 CE/261 AH. His collection was finalized after a prolonged research of fifteen years. It includes 12,000 Traditions.

Bukhari and Muslim, combined together, are referred to as *"sahihayn,"* which means "two reliable books." Similarly, Imam Bukhari and Imam Muslim are referred to together as *"shaykhayn,"* meaning "two great religious scholars." A Tradition which is common in Bukhari and Muslim is termed *"muttafaqun alalh."* It means a Tradition which is "agreed upon" by Imam Bukhari as well as Imam Muslim. Such an agreed upon Tradition is considered to be most trustworthy.

Jami Tirmidi: The third famed *ahadith* book in the six sound series is that of Tirmidi. Its compiler is Imam Abu Isa Muhammad ibn Isa, also known as Imam Tirmidi. He was a well-known disciple of Imam Bukhari. He was born in 824 CE/209 AH in Tirmid, a famous town in Iran. He died in the same town in 892 CE/279 AH. Tirmidi's work contains 2,028 Traditions. Muslim scholars have great regard for this valuable source of a great wisdom.

Sunan Abu Daud: The fourth book in this famous series is known as *Sunan Daud*. The name of the compiler is Abu Daud Sulayman ibn Abbas. He is also known as Imam Abu Daud. He was born in 817 CE/202 AH in Sajistan, a place near Qandhar, then part of Iran. He died in 888 CE/275 AH at the age of seventy-three. *Sunan Abu Daud* consists of 4,800 Traditions.

Sunan Nisai: This is the fifth famous collection in the same series. Imam Abu Abd al-Rahman Ahmad ibn Shuayb Nisai is its compiler. His short name is Imam Nisai. He was born in 830 CE/215 AH in Nisa, a famed town of Iran. He died in 915 CE/303 AH. His book contains 5,761 Traditions.

Sunan ibn Majah: The last among the six sound books is the *Sunan ibn Majah*. It was compiled by Imam Abu Abd Allah Muhammad ibn Yazid ibn Majah. He is also known as Imam ibn Majah. He was born in 824 CE/209 AH in Qazvin, a town in Iran. He died in 886 CE/273 AH after attaining the age of sixty-four. His compilation comprises 4,000 Traditions.

Let's find out what you have learned from

Section 7: The Six Sound Books

Identification:

1. Name the six sound books.

Clarification:

2. Explain what "agreed upon" means.

Section 8: Other Famous Compilations of Traditions

In addition to these famed *ahadith* collections, a large number of other compilations have also been published from time to time. Of these the three widely known ones, several Traditions out of which have been cited in the present book, are as follows: (1) *Sunan Darimi*, (2) *Sunan Bayhaqi*, (3) *Mishkat al-Masabih*.

Sunan Darimi: Its compiler is Imam Abu Muhammad Abd Allah bin Abd al-Rahman al-Darimi. He is also known as Imam Darimi. He was born in 797 CE/181 AH in Samarqand, Central Asia which was then part of Iran. He died in 868 CE/255 AH. He enjoys great reputation for his sound character and vast knowledge. His collection contains 3,550 Traditions.

Sunan Bayhaqi: This collection was compiled by Imam Abu Bakr Ahmad ibn al-Husayn al-Bayhaq. He was born in 994 CE/384 AH in Bayhaq, a village near Nishapur in Iran. He died in 1065 CE/458 AH. Imam Bayhaqi was dedicated to the production of sound religious literature. He is author of about one thousand standard books and scholarly papers.

Mishkat al-Masabih: Its compiler is Imam Wali al-din Abu Abd Allah ibn Abd Allah al-Khatib al-Tabrizi, also known as Imam Tabrizi. He ranks as one of the most eminent *ahadith* scholars of the eighth century AH. Khatib Tabrizi was born in 1030 CE/421 AH in Tabriz, a well-known town in Iran. The date of his death is 1108 CE/502 AH. *Mishkat al-Masabih* contains 5,945 Traditions. The collection is very comprehensive and reliable. At the moment it ranks as the most popular book on *ahadith*. Of all the works on the Traditions, this collection has been consulted most frequently in the preparation of the present book.

Let's find out what you have learned from

Section 8: Other Famous Compilations of Traditions

Identification:

1. Name the three other famous compilations of Traditions referred to by the author in this section.

Clarification:

2. During what centuries were these books compiled?

Section 9: The Main Parts of a Tradition

Let us now understand the basic structure and composition of a Tradition. Every Tradition has three main parts:

    (1) the "*sanad*" or the authority
    (2) the "*matan*" or the text
    (3) the source of where the text is found

Every Tradition starts with the authority. This indicates the original source or the narrator of that particular Tradition. After the authority comes the text which is the original message or the real essence of the Tradition. Following that is the source. An example will clarify the above. Look at the following Tradition:

It is reported by Abd Allah ibn Amr that the Messenger of God (ﷺ) said: Surely the best of you are those who are most excellent in morals. (Agreed upon)

In the above instance, the person mentioned after the Arabic word (from, by) i.e. Abd Allah ibn Amr, is the authority for this particular *hadith* or Tradition. The subsequent matter: Surely the best of you are those who are most excellent in morals, is the text. The words written at the end of the Tradition refer to the source or compiler of the collection. In the above case it is a Tradition "agreed upon" by Muslim and Bukhari. This means that it has been mentioned in the famed *ahadith* books of both of these great scholars.

Let's find out what you have learned from

Section 9: The Main Parts of a Tradition

Identification:

1. The three basic parts of a Tradition are?

Discussion:

2. Discuss with your classmates the knowledge you have gained about the Traditions from this chapter.

Section Answers:

Section 1: Fountain of Wisdom and Guidance

1. 610 CE/13 BH
2. 570 CE/53 BH

Section 2: Muhammad (☝) Inspires All of Humanity

1. The Companions, *ashab*.
2. The Successors, *tabyun*.

Section 3: Main Varieties of Traditions and the Earliest Collections

1. al-Sadiq.
2. (a) The narration of all those words that the Prophet uttered from time to time; (b) the collection of specific instructions and advice which he offered for the guidance of humanity; (c) the statements of all the deeds that he performed in the presence of his Companions and followers; (d) other details of his personal life as witnessed and reported by the members of his family.

Section 4: Developments During the Early Caliphate

1. Abu Bakr al-Siddiq; Umar al-Faruq; Uthman al-Affan; Ali ibn Abi Talib
2. Umar ibn Abd al-Aziz

Section 5: Imam Malik's Decorated Flower Vase

1. *Muwatta*
2. "The decorated."

Section 6: The Musnad of Imam Hanbal

1. *Musnad*.

Section 7: The Six Sound Books

1. *Sahih Bukhari, Sahih Muslim, Jami Tirmidi, Sunan Abu Daud, Sunan Nisai, Sunan ibn Majah*.
2. A Tradition which is agreed upon by both Imam Bukhari and Imam Muslim.

Section 8: Other Famous Compilations of Traditions

1. *Sunan Darimi, Sunan Bayhaqi, Mishkat al-Masabih*
2. *Mishkat al-Masabih*
3. 3rd-5th AH

Section 9: The Main Parts of a Tradition

1. *Sanad* or the authority and *matan* or text and the source of where it is found.
2. Answers vary.

3
The Islamic Way of Life

Section 1: Introduction

What is Islam? Who are Muslims? What do Muslims say and do? This chapter presents those simple Traditions of the Prophet which describe the advantages of becoming a Muslim, the five fundamental principles of Islam and the main qualities of a Muslim. These selected Traditions offer the right guidance about the above matters under the following headings:

Section 2: The Benefits of Becoming a Muslim

Islam is a revolutionary religion. Its acceptance brings success and salvation in all fields of life. The very literal meaning of the word Islam is peace. Islam is a message of peace and prosperity, health and happiness for the whole world because when practiced correctly everyone and everything acts according to its innate nature (*fitra*), following God's will to worship God alone. If you practice the Islamic way of life it is sure to develop your character and personality. You will feel far more happy and be far more successful in life.

Section 3: Five Revolutionary Principles of Islam

Islam's fundamental principles possess the magic powers of changing and reforming people. They provide revolutionary guidance for all individuals and all nations.

Section 4: Love and Respect for the Prophet

Prophet Muhammad (ﷺ) was the greatest benefactor of all humanity in general and of all children in particular. Love and respect for him are a part and parcel of every Muslim's life.

Section 5: Who is a hypocrite?

A hypocrite is one who says one thing with his or her tongue and believes something else with the heart while both the sayings as well as the doings of a Muslim should be one and the same thing.

Let's find out what you have learned from

Section 1: Introduction

Identification:

1. What does the word Islam mean?

Discussion:

2. Discuss the five sections as reflections on the Islamic way of life.

Section 2: The Benefits of Becoming a Muslim

عَنْ عَبْدِ اللهِ بْنِ عَمْرو قَالَ
قَالَ رَسُولُ اللهِ صَلَّى اللهُ عَلَيْهِ وَسَلَّمَ
قَدْ أَفْلَحَ مَنْ أَسْلَمَ.

(مُسْلِمٌ)

***It is reported from Abd Allah ibn Amr
that the Messenger of God (ﷺ) said:
Whoever accepts submission to the Will of God (islam)
attains salvation.
(Muslim)***

Let's find out what you have learned from

Section 2: The Benefits of Becoming a Muslim

Identification:

1. What is the authority for this Tradition?
2. What is the text of this Tradition?
3. What is the source of this Tradition?

Section 3: Five Revolutionary Principles of Islam

عَنِ ابْنِ عُمَرَ قَالَ قَالَ رَسُوْلُ
اللهِ صَلَّى اللهُ عَلَيْهِ وَسَلَّمَ بُنِيَ الْإِسْلَامُ
عَلَى خَمْسٍ شَهَادَةِ اَنْ لَآ اِلهَ اِلَّا
اللهُ وَ اَنَّ مُحَمَّدًا عَبْدُهُ وَرَسُوْلُهُ
وَ اِقَامِ الصَّلوةِ وَ اِيْتَاءِ الزَّكوةِ
وَالْحَجِّ وَصَوْمِ رَمَضَانَ ۔

(مُتَّفَقٌ عَلَيْهِ)

Ibn Umar narrates that
the Messenger of God (ﷺ) said:
Islam is founded on five pillars:
1. Bearing witness that there is no god except Allah
and that Muhammad is His Messenger.
2. Offering the prescribed prayer (salat)
3. Payment of the poor-due (zakat)
4. Performing the prescribed pilgrimage (hajj)
5. Performing the prescribed fast (sawm) in Ramadan.
(Agreed upon)

Let's find out what you have learned from

Section 3: Five Revolutionary Principles of Islam

Identification:

1. Name the five revolutionary principles of Islam according to the above Tradition of the Prophet.

Section 4: Love and Respect for the Prophet

عَنْ اَنَسٍ قَالَ قَالَ رَسُوْلُ
اللهِ صَلَّى اللهُ عَلَيْهِ وَسَلَّمَ لَايُؤْمِنُ
اَحَدُكُمْ حَتَّى اَكُوْنَ اَحَبَّ اِلَيْهِ
مِنْ وَّالِدِهِ وَوَلَدِهِ وَالنَّاسِ
اَجْمَعِيْنَ ۔

﴿اَلْبُخَارِىُّ﴾

Anas reports that
the Messenger of God (ﷺ) said:
None of you becomes a believer
unless I am dearer to him than
his father, his son and all of humanity.
(Bukhari)

Let's find out what you have learned from

Section 4: Love and Respect for the Prophet

Discussion:

1. How does the Prophet describe a believer?

Section 5: Who is a hypocrite?

عَنْ عَبْدِ اللهِ بِنِ عَمْرٍ وَقَالَ

قَالَ رَسُولُ اللهِ صَلَّى اللهُ عَلَيْهِ وَسَلَّم

اَرْبَعٌ مَنْ كُنَّ فِيهِ كَانَ مُنَافِقًا خَالِصًا

اِذَا اُتُّمِنَ خَانَ وَ اِذَا حَدَّثَ كَذَبَ

وَ اِذَا عَاهَدَ غَدَرَ وَاِذَا خَاصَمَ فَجَرَ

(مُتَّفَقٌ عَلَيْهِ)

Abd Allah ibn Amr states that
the Messenger of God (ﷺ) said:
Whosoever shall have four (features) shall be a pure hypocrite:
First of all, when he (or she) is given a trust,
he (or she) is unfaithful;
second, when he (or she) talks, he (or she) lies;
third, when he (or she) makes a promise, he (or she) breaks it;
and fourth, when he (or she) fights,
he (or she) abuses the other person.
(Agreed upon)

Let's find out what you have learned from

Section 5: Who is a hypocrite?

Discussion:
1. Discuss the qualities of a hypocrite and how situations have occurred in today's world where leaders manifest these qualities.

Section Answers:

Section 1: Introduction

1. Peace and acting according to our innate nature (*fitra*).
2. Answers vary.

Section 2: The Benefits of Becoming a Muslim

1. Abd Allah ibn Amr.
2. Whoever accepts submission to the Will of God (*islam*) attains salvation.
3. Muslim

Section 3: Five Revolutionary Principles of Islam

1. (a) Bearing witness that there is no god except Allah and Muhammad is His Messenger
   (b) Offering the prescribed prayer
   (c) Payment of the poor-due
   (d) Performing the prescribed pilgrimage
   (e) Performing the prescribed fast

Section 4: Love and Respect for the Prophet

1. Answers vary.

Section 5: Who is a hypocrite?

1. Answers vary.

4
The Pleasures of Greeting Others

Section 1: Introduction

This chapter gives an idea of the most pleasant and the most healthy manners of wishing and greeting each other. Summaries of the three main sections of the chapter are as follows:

Section 2: Greetings and Salutations

How essential is it to wish each other the decent way. Do not wait for the other one to begin. You wish first. That is the Prophet's way of greeting. When some body offers you good wishes, hasten to present better greetings in return.

Section 3: Give a Hearty Handshake!

Give a hearty handshake when meeting friends. It cements brotherly ties and removes many misunderstandings.

Section 4: Cheerful Smile

Smile cheerfully when you greet people. That is yet another good thing a Muslim has been advised to do.

Try to enjoy the beauty of these manners. Practice them in everyday dealings. You will then feel far more cheerful and far more healthy

Let's find out what you have learned from

Section 1: Introduction

Identification:

1. What are the three ways given by the author from the Traditions about greeting others?
2. Discuss whether or not you follow the Prophet's guidance in greeting others.

Section 2: Greetings and Salutations

عَنْ اَبِي هُرَيْرَةَ قَالَ   قَالَ
رَسُولُ اللهِ صَلَّى اللهُ عَلَيْهِ وَسَلَّمَ
اَفْشُوا السَّلَامَ بَيْنَكُمْ.

(مُسْلِمٌ)

Abu Hurayra narrates that
the Messenger of God (ﷺ) said:
Greet each other when you meet.
(Muslim)

عَنْ عَبْدِ اللهِ بْنِ عَمْرٍو اَنَّ
رَجُلًا سَأَلَ رَسُولَ اللهِ صَلَّى اللهُ عَلَيْهِ
وَسَلَّمَ اَيُّ الْاِسْلَامِ خَيْرٌ قَالَ تُطْعِمُ
الطَّعَامَ وَتَقْرَى السَّلَامَ عَلَى مَنْ
عَرَفْتَ وَمَنْ لَّمْ تَعْرِفْ.

(مُتَّفَقٌ عَلَيْهِ)

Abd Allah ibn Amr reported that a man asked
the Messenger of God (ﷺ): What is the best in Islam?
(The Messenger) said: Your feeding (the poor)
and offering salutations to a person you know
and to a person you do not know.
(Agreed upon)

عَنْ اَنَسٍ اَنَّ رَسُوْلَ اللهِ صَلَّى
اللهُ عَلَيْهِ وَسَلَّمَ قَالَ يَا بُنَيَّ اِذَا دَخَلْتَ
عَلَى اَهْلِكَ فَسَلِّمْ يَكُوْنُ بَرَكَةً عَلَيْكَ
وَعَلَى اَهْلِ بَيْتِكَ ـ

‏(التِّرْمِذِيُّ)

Anas states that
the Messenger of God (ﷺ) said:
My dear son! Greet the inhabitants when you enter your home.
This shall yield blessings for you and for your family.
(Tirmidi)

عَنْ قَتَادَةَ قَالَ قَالَ النَّبِيُّ
صَلَّى اللهُ عَلَيْهِ وَسَلَّمَ اِذَا دَخَلْتُمْ
بَيْتًا فَسَلِّمُوْا عَلَى اَهْلِهِ وَ اِذَا
خَرَجْتُمْ فَاَوْدِعُوْا اَهْلَهُ بِسَلَامٍ ـ

‏(الْبَيْهَقِيُّ)

Qatadah narrates that
the Messenger of God (ﷺ) said:
When you enter a house, greet its inhabitants
and when you leave, depart with salutations.
(Bayhaqi)

عَنْ جَابِرٍ قَالَ قَالَ رَسُولُ اللهِ
صَلَّى اللهُ عَلَيْهِ وَسَلَّمَ السَّلَامُ قَبْلَ ٱلْكَلَامِ
(ٱلتِّرْمِذِيُّ)

Jaber reports that
the Messenger of God (ﷺ) said:
Greet each other before speaking.
(Tirmidi)

عَنْ اَبِىْ هُرَيْرَةَ قَالَ قَالَ رَسُولُ
اللهِ صَلَّى اللهُ عَلَيْهِ وَسَلَّمَ يُسَلِّمُ
ٱلصَّغِيْرُ عَلَى ٱلْكَبِيْرِ وَ ٱلْمَارُّ عَلَى ٱلْقَاعِدِ
وَٱلْقَلِيْلُ عَلَى ٱلْكَثِيْرِ ۔

(مُتَّفَقٌ عَلَيْهِ)

Abu Hurayra states that
the Messenger of God (ﷺ) said:
The younger should greet the older,
the walking should greet those sitting
and the smaller group should greet the larger one.
(Agreed upon)

عَنْ اَبِىْ اُمَامَةَ قَالَ قَالَ رَسُوْلُ اللهِ صَلَّى اللهُ عَلَيْهِ وَسَلَّمَ اِنَّ اَوْلَى النَّاسِ بِاللهِ مَنْ بَدَءَ بِالسَّلَامِ ۔

(اَحْمَدُ وَالتِّرْمِذِىُّ وَاَبُوْدَاوُدَ)

**Abu Umama reports that
the Messenger of God (ﷺ) said:
He who greets first is nearest to God.
(Ahmad, Tirmidi and Abu Daud)**

عَنْ عَبْدِ اللهِ عَنِ النَّبِىِّ صَلَّى اللهُ عَلَيْهِ وَ سَلَّمَ قَالَ الْبَادِئُ بِالسَّلَامِ بَرِئٌ مِنَ الْكِبْرِ ۔

(الْبَيْهَقِىُّ)

**Abd Allah reports that
the Prophet (ﷺ) said:
The initiator in greetings
is free from vanity.
(Bayhaqi)**

عَنْ عِمْرَانَ بْنِ حُصَيْنٍ اَنَّ
رَجُلًا جَآءَ اِلَى النَّبِىِّ صَلَّى اللهُ عَلَيْهِ
وَسَلَّمَ فَقَالَ السَّلَامُ عَلَيْكُمْ ـ فَرَدَّ
عَلَيْهِ ـ ثُمَّ جَلَسَ ـ فَقَالَ النَّبِىُّ صَلَّى
اللهُ عَلَيْهِ وَسَلَّمَ عَشْرٌ ـ ثُمَّ جَآءَ
اٰخَرُ فَقَالَ السَّلَامُ عَلَيْكُمْ وَرَحْمَةُ
اللهِ ـ فَرَدَّ عَلَيْهِ ـ فَجَلَسَ ـ فَقَالَ
عِشْرُوْنَ ـ ثُمَّ جَآءَ اٰخَرُ فَقَالَ
السَّلَامُ عَلَيْكُمْ وَرَحْمَةُ اللهِ وَبَرَكَاتُهُ
فَرَدَّ عَلَيْهِ ـ فَجَلَسَ ـ فَقَالَ ثَلٰثُوْنَ ـ

(التِّرْمِذِىُّ وَاَبُوْدَاوُدَ)

Imran ibn Husayn narrates that
a man came to the Prophet (ﷺ) and said:
Peace be upon you.
The Prophet returned the greetings.
Then he sat down.
The Prophet (ﷺ) said:
Ten (that is, you have earned ten credits of virtue).
Then another person came in and said:
Peace and the mercy of God be upon you.
The Prophet returned the greeting.
He took his seat.
The Prophet then said: Twenty.
Thereafter another man came in and said:
Peace, mercy and the blessings of God be upon you.
The Prophet returned the greetings.
He sat down.
Then the Prophet said: Thirty.
(Tirmidi and Abu Daud)

Let's find out what you have learned from

Section 2: Greetings and Salutations

Discussion:

1. Discuss how important it is for a Muslim to give greetings and salutations to others. How have you felt when someone has not greeted you?

Section 3: Give a Hearty Handshake!

عَنْ اَنَسٍ قَالَ قَالَ رَجُلٌ يَا
رَسُوْلَ اللهِ الرَّجُلُ مِنَّا يَلْقَى اَخَاهُ اَوْ
صَدِيْقَهُ اَيَنْحَنِى لَهُ، قَالَ لَا ـ قَالَ
اَفَيَلْتَزِمُهُ وَ يُقَبِّلَهُ ـ قَالَ لَا ـ
قَالَ اَفَيَأْخُذُ بِيَدِهِ وَ يُصَافِحُهُ
قَالَ نَعَمْ ـ

(التِّرْمِذِىُّ)

Anas states that a man asked:
O Messenger of God!
When someone from amongst us meets his brother or friend,
should he bow his head before him?
(The Messenger) replied: No.
He asked: Should he embrace him or kiss him?
(The Messenger) replied: No.
He asked: Should he shake his hand?
(The Messenger) replied: Yes.
(Tirmidi)

عَنْ عَطَاءِ نِ الْخُرَاسَانِى اَنَّ رَسُوْلَ
اللهِ صَلَّى اللهُ عَلَيْهِ وَسَلَّمَ قَالَ تَصَافَحُوْ
يَذْهَبُ الْغِلَّ ـ

(مَالِكٌ)

Ata al-Khurasani reports that
the Messenger of God (ﷺ) said:
Shake each other's hand. It does away with malice.
(Malik)

عَنِ الْبَرَاءِ بن عَازِبٍ قَالَ قَالَ
النَّبِيُّ صَلَّى اللهُ عَلَيْهِ وَسَلَّمَ مَا مِنْ
مُسْلِمَيْنِ يَلْتَقِيَانِ فَلِيَتَصَافَحَانِ إِلَّا
غُفِرَلَهُمَا قَبْلَ أَنْ يَّتَفَرَّقَا ۔

(اَحْمَدُ وَالتِّرْمِذِيُّ وَابْنُ مَاجَةَ)

Bara ibn Azib states that
the Prophet (ﷺ) said:
Any two Muslims who shake hands on meeting
are forgiven before they part from each other.
(Ahmad, Tirmidi and Ibn Majah)

عَنِ الْبَرَاءِ بن عَازِبٍ قَالَ قَالَ
رَسُولُ اللهِ صَلَّى اللهُ عَلَيْهِ وَسَلَّمَ الْمُسْلِمَانِ
إِذَا تَصَافَحَا لَمْ يَبْقَ بَيْنَهُمَا ذَنْبٌ
إِلَّا سَقَطَ ۔

(الْبَيْهَقِيُّ)

Bara ibn Azib reports that
the Messenger of God (ﷺ) said:
When two Muslims shake hands with each other,
no sin remains between them which is not pardoned.
(Bayhaqi)

عَنْ اَبِيْ اُمَامَةَ اَنَّ رَسُوْلَ اللهِ
صَلَّى اللهُ عَلَيْهِ وَسَلَّمَ قَالَ تَمَامُ تَحِيَّاتِكُمْ
بَيْنَكُمُ الْمُصَافَحَةُ ـ
(اَحْمَدُ وَالتِّرْمِذِيُّ)

Abu Umama narrates that
the Prophet (ﷺ) said:
The perfect way of your mutual greeting
is handshaking.
(Ahmad and Tirmidi)

Let's find out what you have learned from

Section 3: Give a Hearty Handshake!

Discussion:

1. From these Traditions we see how important it is to shake hands with each other when we meet. When is handshaking not recommended in Islam?

Section 4: Cheerful Smile

عَنْ عَبْدِ اللهِ ابْنِ الْحَارِثِ بْنِ جَزْءٍ
قَالَ مَا رَأَيْتُ أَحَدًا أَكْثَرَ تَبَسُّمًا مِنْ
رَسُولِ اللهِ صَلَّى اللهُ عَلَيْهِ وَسَلَّمَ ۔
(التِّرْمِذِيُّ)

Abd Allah ibn Harith ibn Jazaa reports:
I never saw anyone smiling more
than the Messenger of God (ﷺ)
(Tirmidi)

عَنْ عَائِشَةَ قَالَتْ مَا رَأَيْتُ
النَّبِيَّ صَلَّى اللهُ عَلَيْهِ وَسَلَّمَ مُسْتَجْمِعاً
ضَاحِكاً حَتَّى أَرَى مِنْهُ لَهَوَاتِهِ إِنَّمَا
كَانَ يَتَبَسَّمُ ۔
(الْبُخَارِيُّ)

Ayisha narrates:
I have not seen the Prophet (ﷺ)
bursting into such laughter
that I could see his palate.
Rather, he used to smile.
(Bukhari)

Let's find out what you have learned from

Section 4: Cheerful Smile

Discussion:

1. Discuss your feelings about people who are friendly and always have a cheerful smile on their face.

Sections Answers:

Section 1: Introduction

1. Greetings and salutations; giving a hearty handshake and having a cheerful smile.
2. Answers vary.

Section 2: Greetings and Salutations

1. Answers vary.

Section 3: Give a Hearty Handshake

1. Answers vary. It is not recommended for boys and girls or males and females who are not related through close kinship to shake hands.

Section 4: Cheerful Smile

1. Answers vary.

5
Seeking Knowledge and Wisdom

Section 1: Introduction

Acquiring knowledge and skill is essential for every one living in the modern world. It is useful as well as pleasant to pursue knowledge. Prophet Muhammad (ﷺ) laid strong emphasis on getting and spreading useful knowledge and wisdom.

The Traditions presented in this chapter explain the following points:

Section 2: Religiously Obligatory for Every Muslim

Seeking of knowledge is religiously obligatory for every Muslim, boy or girl, man or woman.

Section 3: Travel for Knowledge and Learning

Acquisition of knowledge and learning may involve travel. One should not hesitate visiting any part of the world for the sake of education.

Section 4: The Conduct of a Student

In the Muslim way of life knowing and learning are virtuous pursuits. A student should, therefore, refrain from all sorts of undesirable activities.

The above instructions hold equally good about the knowledge you are acquiring now and the knowledge you may seek in later years.

Let's find out what you have learned from

Section 1: Introduction

Discussion:

1. Discuss the importance of gaining knowledge and how knowledge of something has helped you.

Section 2: Religiously Obligatory for Every Muslim

عَنْ اَنَسٍ قَالَ قَالَ رَسُوْلُ اللهِ
صَلَّى اللهُ عَلَيْهِ وَسَلَّمَ طَلَبُ الْعِلْمِ
فَرِيْضَةٌ عَلٰى كُلِّ مُسْلِمٍ وَّمُسْلِمَةٍ ۔
(اِبْنُ مَاجَةَ)

Anas said that
the Messenger of God (ﷺ) said:
Seeking of knowledge is
obligatory upon
every male and female Muslim.
(Ibn Majah)

Let's find out what you have learned from

Section 2: Religiously Obligatory for Every Muslim

Discussion:

1. Discuss what it means in Islam for something to be obligatory. What besides gaining knowledge is obligatory in Islam?

Section 2: Travel for Knowledge and Learning

عَنْ اَبِیْ هُرَیْرَةَ قَالَ قَالَ رَسُوْلُ اللهِ
صَلَّی اللهُ عَلَیْهِ وَسَلَّمَ کَلِمَةُ الْحِکْمَةِ
ضَآلَّةُ الْمُؤْمِنِ فَحَیْثُ وَجَدَهَا فَهُوَ
اَحَقُّ بِهَا ۔

(التِّرْمِذِیُّ)

Abu Hurayra reports that
the Messenger of God (ﷺ) said:
A word of wisdom is the lost property of the believer
so wherever the believer finds it,
he (or she) has the best right to it.
(Tirmidi)

Let's find out what you have learned from

Section 3: Travel for Knowledge and Learning

Discussion:

1. What a beautiful thought—whenever we hear a word of wisdom it belongs to us as believers and is said by the Prophet to be property we have lost. Discuss this with your classmates.

Section 4: The Conduct of a Student

عَنْ اَنَسٍ قَالَ قَالَ رَسُوْلُ اللهِ
صَلَّى اللهُ عَلَيْهِ وَسَلَّمَ مَنْ خَرَجَ
فِىْ طَلَبِ الْعِلْمِ فَهُوَ فِىْ سَبِيْلِ اللهِ
حَتّٰى يَرْجِعَ -

(التِّرْمِذِىُّ وَالدَّارِىُّ)

*It is reported by Anas that
the Messenger of God (ﷺ) said:
Whoever goes out to seek knowledge
is on God's path until he (or she) returns.
(Tirmidi and Darimi)*

Let's find out what you have learned from
Section 4: The Conduct of a Student

Discussion:

1. Discuss with your classmates this sacred concept in Islam that the seeking of knowledge is a sign of being on God's path.

Section Answers:

Section 1: Introduction

1. Answers vary.

Section 2: Religiously Obligatory for Every Muslim

1. Answers vary.

Section 3: Travel for Knowledge and Learning

1. Answers vary.

Section 4: The Conduct of a Student

1. Answers vary.

6
Health and Cleanliness

Section 1: Introduction

Personal health and environmental cleanliness occupy a central position in the Muslim way of life. Prophet Muhammad (ﷺ) offered practical guidance about all aspects of human health and happiness.

The present chapter discusses the basic health and hygiene matters under three sections:

Section 2: Bathroom Manners

This section presents some useful instructions regarding the use of the bathroom when answering the call of nature.

Section 3: Advantages of Brushing Our Teeth

Traditions in the second section of this chapter highlight the necessity and utility of brushing our teeth regularly. The Prophet was himself extremely punctual about cleansing his teeth. He advised his followers to be conscious of dental health.

Section 4: Taking a Bath

The why, where, when and how of taking a bath are briefly dealt with in the last section.

You will realize that these fundamental principles of health and hygiene are extremely useful for everyone. If you start acting on them you are sure to enjoy sound health for the whole of your life.

Let's find out what you have learned from

Section 1: Introduction

Discussion:

1. Discuss how these Traditions of the Prophet are what modern day classes on hygiene teach us and how they differ.

Section 2: Bathroom Manners

عَنْ سَلْمَانَ قَالَ نَهْنَا يَعْنِى
رَسُوْلُ اللهِ صَلَّى اللهُ عَلَيْهِ وَسَلَّمَ اَنْ
نَسْتَقْبِلَ الْقِبْلَةَ لِغَائِطٍ اَوْبَوْلٍ ۔

(مُسْلِمٌ)

It is reported by Salman that
the Messenger of God (ﷺ)
forbade us to face the Kabah
while defecating or urinating.
(Muslim)

عَنْ اَبِىْ اَيُّوْبَ الْاَنْصَارِىِّ قَالَ
قَالَ رَسُوْلُ اللهِ صَلَّى اللهُ عَلَيْهِ وَسَلَّمَ
اِذَا اَتَيْتُمُ الْغَائِطَ فَلَا تَسْتَقْبِلُوا
الْقِبْلَةَ وَلَا تَسْتَدْبِرُوْهَا وَلٰكِنْ
شَرِّقُوْا اَوْ غَرِّبُوْا ۔

(مُتَّفَقٌ عَلَيْهِ)

Abu Ayyub Ansari states that
the Messenger of God (ﷺ) said:
When you go to the bathroom
do not turn your face nor your back towards the Kabah.
Rather face towards the East or the West.
(Agreed upon)

Let's find out what you have learned from

Section 2: Bathroom Manners

Discussion:

1. These two Traditions on bathroom manners are not taught in classes on hygiene but are essential to a Muslim who follows the *Sunnah* of the Prophet. We may not know the reason why the Prophet tells us we should not face the Kabah or have our back towards it when answering the call of nature, but we do so because he did so. We cannot go wrong if we follow his model. Discuss this with your class.

Section 3: Advantages of Brushing Our Teeth

عَنْ عَآئِشَةَ قَالَتْ قَالَ رَسُوْلُ
اللهِ صَلَّى اللهُ عَلَيْهِ وَسَلَّمَ السِّوَاكُ
مَطْهَرَةٌ لِلْفَمِ مَرْضَاةٌ لِلرَّبِّ ۔

(اَلْبُخَارِيُّ وَالشَّافِعِيُّ وَاَحْمَدُ وَالدَّارِمِيُّ وَالنَّسَائِيُّ)

It is reported by Ayisha that
the Messenger of God (ﷺ) said:
Brushing (our) teeth purifies the mouth.
It is a means of seeking the Lord's pleasure.
(Bukhari, Shafii, Ahmad, Darimi and Nisai)

عَنْ شُرَيْحِ بْنِ هَانِئٍ قَالَ
سَاَلْتُ عَآئِشَةَ بِاَيِّ شَيْءٍ كَانَ يَبْدَءُ
رَسُوْلُ اللهِ صَلَّى اللهُ عَلَيْهِ وَسَلَّمَ اِذَا
دَخَلَ بَيْتَهُ ۔ قَالَتْ بِالسِّوَاكِ ۔

(مُسْلِمٌ)

Surayh ibn Hani narrates that he asked Ayisha:
What was the first thing the Messenger of God (ﷺ) did
when he entered his home?
She replied: Brush his teeth.
(Muslim)

Let's find out what you have learned from

Section 3: Advantages of Brushing Our Teeth

Identification:

1. What does the Prophet use to brush his teeth?

Clarification:

2. Note that there are five sources for the Tradition on the top of page 54. What does this tell you?

3. If someone were to ask you, "What is the first thing you do when you enter your home?" What would you say?

Section 4: Taking a Bath

عَنْ اَبِىْ مَالِكِ بِالاَشْعَرِيِّ قَالَ
قَالَ رَسُوْلُ اللهِ صَلَّى اللهُ عَلَيْهِ وَسَلَّمَ
اَلطَّهُوْرُ شَطْرُ الْاِيْمَانِ ۔

(مُسْلِمٌ)

Abu Malik al-Ashari reports that
the Messenger of God (ﷺ) said:
Cleanliness is half of faith.
(Muslim)

عَنْ اَبِىْ هُرَيْرَةَ قَالَ قَالَ رَسُوْلُ
اللهِ صَلَّى اللهُ عَلَيْهِ وَسَلَّمَ حَقٌّ عَلَى
كُلِّ مُسْلِمٍ اَنْ يَّغْتَسِلَ فِىْ كُلِّ سَبْعَةِ
اَيَّامٍ يَوْمًا يَغْسِلُ فِيْهِ رَأْسَهُ وَجَسَدَهُ ۔

(مُتَّفَقٌ عَلَيْهِ)

It is stated by Abu Hurayra that
the Messenger of God (ﷺ) said:
It is obligatory for every Muslim to take a bath once in every
seven days (at least) and then wash his (or her) head and the
whole of his (or her) body.
(Agreed upon)

عَنِ ابْنِ عُمَرَ قَالَ قَالَ رَسُوْلُ
اللهِ صَلَّى اللهُ عَلَيْهِ وَسَلَّمَ إِذَا جَاءَ
أَحَدُكُمُ الْجُمُعَةَ فَلْيَغْتَسِلْ ۔

(مُتَّفَقٌ عَلَيْهِ)

Ibn Umar reports that
the Messenger of God (ﷺ) said:
Whoever of you goes to the Friday prayer
should take a bath beforehand.
(Agreed upon)

عَنِ ابْنِ عَبَّاسٍ قَالَ كَانَ
رَسُوْلُ اللهِ صَلَّى اللهُ عَلَيْهِ وَسَلَّمَ
يَغْتَسِلُ يَوْمَ الْفِطْرِ وَ يَوْمَ الْاَضْحَى ۔

(ابْنُ مَاجَةَ)

It is reported by Ibn Abbas that
the Messenger of God (ﷺ)
used to take a bath on the day of the Festival of fitr
(marking the end of the month of Ramadan),
and the Festival of adha (sacrifice).
(Ibn Majah)

عَنْ يَعْلَى قَالَ إِنَّ رَسُولَ اللهِ صَلَّى
اللهُ عَلَيْهِ وَسَلَّمَ رَأَى رَجُلًا يَغْتَسِلُ
بِالْبَرَازِ ۔ فَصَعِدَ الْمِنْبَرَ فَحَمِدَ اللهَ
وَأَثْنَى عَلَيْهِ ۔ ثُمَّ قَالَ إِنَّ اللهَ
حَيِيٌّ سَتِيرٌ يُحِبُّ الْحَيَاءَ وَالتَّسَتُّرَ
فَإِذَا اغْتَسَلَ أَحَدُكُمْ فَلْيَسْتَتِرْ ۔

(رَأَبُوْدَاؤُدَ وَالنَّسَائِيُّ)

Yaala narrates that
the Messenger of God (ﷺ)
saw a man bathing (naked) in an open place.
He ascended the pulpit and praised and glorified God.
Then he said: Surely God is the possessor of
modesty and concealer of faults.
He loves modesty and concealment
so when any one of you takes a bath,
let him (or her) conceal himself (or herself) from others.
(Abu Daud and Nisai)

Let's find out what you have learned from

Section 4: Taking a Bath

Discussion:

1. There are some rural and city places in the world where clean water is scarce so the Prophet advised a weekly bath. Does this mean that if we have clean water available and can bathe more often we should not do so? Discuss this with your class.

Section Answers:

Section 1: Introduction

1. Answers vary.

Section 2: Bathroom Manners

1. Answers vary.

Section 3: Advantages of Brushing Our Teeth

1. *Miswak*.
2. It speaks to the reliability of a Tradition.
3. Answers vary.

Section 4: Taking a Bath

1. Answers vary.

7
Eating, Drinking and Entertaining

Section 1: Introduction

What are civilized eating manners? What is the best way to drink water, for instance? How are guests to be honored and entertained? Knowledge about these matters adds to the pleasures of living. Prophet Muhammad (ﷺ) has useful guidance to offer in this field as well. Needless to say that the health and happiness of the individual and of the society depend considerably on proper eating habits, decent drinking manners and generous Traditions of hospitality. The above issues have been explained in this chapter under the following four sections:

Section 2: How to Begin Eating
This section gives a brief account of the Islamic way of starting to eat.

Section 3: On Finishing the Meal
What is the graceful way of winding up your meals? Section three offers a few Traditions pertaining to the formalities to be observed when one has finished eating.

Section 4: Manners in Drinking
A Muslim must drink decently. The Prophet compares a crude drinking habit to a camel's drinking style. This section summarizes the Muslim manners of drinking.

Section 5: Hospitality and Entertainment
Islam lays great emphasis on hospitality. It is fine to invite people and to eat with them. Showing every respect to guests and seeing them off properly after entertaining them have been highly prized by the Prophet. The last section focuses on all such social etiquettes in the light of a few interesting Traditions.

Let's find out what you have learned from

Section 1: Introduction

Discussion:

1. Does there appear to be anything outdated in these sections? How does it help us to follow the Prophet's Traditions on eating, drinking and entertaining? Does it harm us in any way?

Section 2: How to Begin Eating

عَنْ عُمَرَ بْنِ اَبِى سَلَمَةَ قَالَ
كُنْتُ غُلَامًا فِى حَجْرِ رَسُوْلِ اللهِ صَلَّى
اللهُ عَلَيْهِ وَسَلَّمَ وَكَانَتْ يَدِىْ تَطِيْشُ
فِى الصَّحْفَةِ ـ فَقَالَ لِى رَسُوْلُ اللهِ صَلَّى
اللهُ عَلَيْهِ وَسَلَّمَ سَمِّ اللهَ وَ كُلْ
بِيَمِيْنِكَ وَكُلْ مِمَّا يَلِيْكَ ـ

(مُتَّفَقٌ عَلَيْهِ)

Umar ibn Abu Salmah states:
I was a boy under the care of the Messenger of God (ﷺ).
My hand was moving fast in the bowl, taking from every side.
The Messenger of God (ﷺ) said to me:
Say: In the Name of God. Eat with your right hand and eat from the side nearest to you.
(Agreed upon)

عَنْ عَائِشَةَ قَالَتْ قَالَ رَسُوْلُ اللهِ
صَلَّى اللهُ عَلَيْهِ وَسَلَّمَ اِذَا اَكَلَ اَحَدُكُمْ
فَنَسِىَ اَنْ يَّذْكُرَ اللهَ عَلَى طَعَامِهِ
فَلْيَقُلْ بِسْمِ اللهِ اَوَّلَهُ وَاٰخِرَهُ ـ

(اَلتِّرْمِذِىُّ وَاَبُوْدَاؤُدَ)

It is reported by Ayisha that
the Messenger of God (ﷺ) said: When any one of you eats
but forgets to remember God's Name over his food,
let him say: 'In the Name of God'
from the beginning to the end.
(Tirmidi and Abu Daud)

عَنِ ابْنِ عُمَرَ قَالَ قَالَ رَسُوْلُ
اللهِ صَلَّى اللهُ عَلَيْهِ وَسَلَّمَ لَا يَاْكُلَنَّ
اَحَدُكُمْ بِشِمَالِهِ وَلَا يَشْرَبَنَّ بِهَا
فَاِنَّ الشَّيْطَنَ يَاْكُلُ بِشِمَالِهِ وَ
يَشْرَبُ بِهَا ۔

(مُسْلِمٌ)

**Ibn Umar reports that
the Messenger of God (ﷺ) said: When any one of you eats,
let him eat with his right hand and when he drinks,
let him drink with his right hand.**
(Muslim)

عَنْ اَنَس قَالَ قَالَ رَسُوْلُ اللهِ
صَلَّى اللهُ عَلَيْهِ وَسَلَّمَ اِنَّ اللهَ تَعَالَى
لَيَرْضَى عَنِ الْعَبْدِ اَنْ يَاْكُلَ الْاَ كْلَةَ
فَيَحْمَدُهُ عَلَيْهَا اَوْ يَشْرَبَ الشَّرْبَةَ
فَيَحْمَدُهُ عَلَيْهَا ۔

(مُسْلِمٌ)

**Anas reports that
the Messenger of God (ﷺ) said:
Verily God is certainly pleased
with a person who takes food
and then praises God for it
or takes drink
and praises God for the same.**
(Muslim)

عَنْ اَبِىْ حُجَيْفَةَ قَالَ قَالَ النَّبِىُّ
صَلَّى اللهُ عَلَيْهِ وَسَلَّمَ لَا اٰكُلُ مُتَّكِئًا

(اَلْبُخَارِىُّ)

**It is stated by Abu Hurayra that
the Prophet (ﷺ) said:
I do not eat in a reclining position.
(Bukhari)**

Let's find out what you have learned from

Section 4: How to Begin Eating

Clarification:

1. What three things about eating does the Prophet tell us in the first Tradition in this section?
2. Who is God pleased with according to the Tradition on the bottom of page 63?

Section 3: On Finishing the Meal

عَنْ اَبِیْ هُرَیْرَةَ قَالَ قَالَ
رَسُوْلُ اللهِ صَلَّى اللهُ عَلَیْهِ وَسَلَّمَ
الطَّاعِمُ الشَّاكِرُ كَالصَّائِمِ الصَّابِرِ

(اَلتِّرْمِذِیُّ وَابْنُ مَاجَةَ وَالدَّارِمِیُّ)

Abu Hurayra reports that
the Messenger of God (ﷺ) said:
A person who is thankful when eating
is like a person who fasts patiently.
(Tirmidi, Ibn Majah and Darimi)

عَنْ اَبِیْ سَعِیْدِنِ الْخُدْرِیّ قَالَ
كَانَ رَسُوْلُ اللهِ صَلَّى اللهُ عَلَیْهِ وَسَلَّمَ
اِذَا فَرَغَ مِنْ طَعَامِهٖ قَالَ اَلْحَمْدُ
لِلّٰهِ الَّذِیْ اَطْعَمَنَا وَسَقَانَا وَجَعَلَنَا
مُسْلِمِیْنَ ۔

(اَلتِّرْمِذِیُّ وَاَبُوْدَاؤُدَ وَابْنُ مَاجَةَ)

It is reported by Abu Said al-Khudri that
when the Messenger of God (ﷺ)
finished his meals, he used to say:
All praise is for the Lord Who gave us to eat
and to drink and made us Muslims.
(Tirmidi, Abu Daud and Ibn Majah)

عَنْ مُعَاذِ بْنِ اَنَسٍ اَنَّ رَسُوْلَ
اللهِ صَلَّى اللهُ عَلَيْهِ وَسَلَّمَ قَالَ مَنْ
اَكَلَ طَعَامًا ثُمَّ قَالَ الْحَمْدُ لِلّهِ الَّذِى
اَطْعَمَنِيْ هٰذَا الطَّعَامَ وَرَزَقَنِيْهِ مِنْ
غَيْرِ حَوْلٍ مِنِّيْ وَلَا قُوَّةٍ غُفِرَلَهُ
مَا تَقَدَّمَ مِنْ ذَنْبِهِ -

(اَلتِّرْمِذِىُّ)

Muaz ibn Anas narrates that
the Messenger of God (ﷺ) said:
All the preceding sins are pardoned
of a person who eats food and then says:
All praise be to God Who gave me the food to eat
and made it accessible to me
without any effort on my part.
(Tirmidi)

Let's find out what you have learned from

Section 3: On Finishing the Meal

Identification:

1. What did the Prophet say when he finished his meals?

Clarification:

2. How is a person who is thankful when eating like a person who fasts patiently?

Section 4: Manners of Drinking

عَنِ ابْنِ عَبَّاسٍ قَالَ قَالَ رَسُولُ
اللهِ صَلَّى اللهُ عَلَيْهِ وَسَلَّمَ لَا تَشْرَبُوا
وَاحِدًا كَشُرْبِ الْبَعِيرِ وَلٰكِنِ اشْرَبُوا
مَثْنٰى وَثُلٰثَ وَسَمُّوا إِذَا أَنْتُمْ
شَرِبْتُمْ وَاحْمَدُوا إِذَا أَنْتُمْ
رَفَعْتُمْ ۔

(التِّرْمِذِيُّ)

It is reported by Ibn Abbas that
the Messenger of God (ﷺ) said:
Don't drink in one breath like a camel drinks,
but drink with two or three (pauses).
Say 'In the Name of God' when you start drinking
and 'All praise for God'
when you finish.
(Tirmidi)

عَنْ أَنَسٍ قَالَ كَانَ رَسُولُ اللهِ
صَلَّى اللهُ عَلَيْهِ وَسَلَّمَ يَتَنَفَّسُ فِى
الشَّرَابِ ثَلٰثًا ۔

(مُتَّفَقٌ عَلَيْهِ)

Anas reported that
the Messenger of God (ﷺ)
used to take three breaths for one drink.
(Agreed upon)

عَنْ اَبِىْ سَعِيْدٍ لِلْخُدْرِىّ اَنَّ
النَّبِىَّ صَلَّى اللهُ عَلَيْهِ وَسَلَّمَ نَهٰى
عَنِ النَّفْخِ فِى الشَّرَابِ ۔

(لِلتِّرْمِذِىّ وَالدَّارِمِىّ)

Abu Said al-Khudri stated that
the Prophet (ﷺ)
prohibited exhaling while drinking.
(Tirmidi and Darimi)

Let's find out what you have learned from

Section 4: Manners of Drinking

Discussion:

1. How do we begin and end drinking something?
2. Discuss how the Traditions help us in drinking liquids.

Section 5: Hospitality and Entertainment

عَنْ عُمَرَ بْنِ الْخَطَّابِ قَالَ قَالَ
رَسُولُ اللهِ صَلَّى اللهُ عَلَيْهِ وَسَلَّمَ كُلُوا
جَمِيعًا وَلَا تَفَرَّقُوا فَإِنَّ الْبَرَكَةَ
مَعَ الْجَمَاعَةِ.

(رَابْنُ مَاجَةَ)

Umar ibn al-Khattab states that
the Messenger of God (ﷺ) said:
Eat together and not separately
because blessing comes
when eating in the company of others.
(Ibn Majah)

عَنْ أَبِي هُرَيْرَةَ قَالَ قَالَ رَسُولُ اللهِ
صَلَّى اللهُ عَلَيْهِ وَسَلَّمَ مَنْ كَانَ يُؤْمِنُ
بِاللهِ وَالْيَوْمِ الْآخِرِ فَلْيُكْرِمْ ضَيْفَهُ.

(مُتَّفَقٌ عَلَيْهِ)

Abu Hurayra reports that
the Messenger of God (ﷺ) said:
Whoever believes in God and the Last Day
should honor his guest.
(Agreed upon)

عَنْ اَبِى هُرَيْرَةَ قَالَ قَالَ رَسُوْلُ
اللهِ صَلَّى اللهُ عَلَيْهِ وَسَلَّمَ مِنَ السُّنَّةِ
اَنْ يَّخْرُجَ الرَّجُلُ مَعَ ضَيْفِهِ اِلَى
بَابِ الدَّارِ۔

(ابْنُ مَاجَةَ وَالْبَيْهَقِيُّ)

Abu Hurayra states that
the Messenger of God (ﷺ) said:
It is the Sunnah (Prophet's way of life)
that a person should accompany his guest
up to the door of his house.
(Ibn Majah and Bayhaqi)

Let's find out what you have learned from

Section 5: Hospitality and Entertainment

Discussion:

1. Discuss the importance of eating with others.
2. Discuss how we show hospitality according to the last two Traditions in this section.

Section Answers:

Section 1: Introduction

1. Answers vary.

Section 2: How to Begin Eating

1. Say: In the Name of God before we eat and eat with our right hand and from the side of the plate nearest us.
2. One who praises God for food and drink.

Section 3: On Finishing the Meal

1. All praise is for the Lord Who gave us to eat and to drink and made us Muslims or all praise be to God Who gave me the food to eat and made it accessible to me without any effort on my part.

Section 4: Manners of Drinking

1. We begin with 'In the Name of God' (*bismillah*) and end with 'All praise for God' (*al-hamdullah*).
2. Answers vary.

Section 5: Hospitality and Entertainment

1. Answers vary.
2. Answers vary.

8
Our Dress and Appearance

Section 1: Introduction

What is a modest dress? What is a graceful form? What should decent men and women look like? What are the real qualities of covering our human form? Guidance about the above matters is available in the following two sections of this chapter:

Section 2: The Modest Dress

The first section presents Traditions highlighting the merits and demerits of good and bad clothes. The Prophet always preferred wearing simple, clean and graceful clothes.

Section 3: Our Form and Appearance

Maintaining a dignified outward form is equally significant. The Islamic way of life rules out disfiguration of the human shape. No one is allowed to keep his hair disorderly nor display bad taste in appearance. The Traditions in this chapter show that the dress of a person must be simple, clean and tidy. Similarly, the general appearance of boys and girls, men and women, must be graceful and dignified.

Let's find out what you have learned from

Section 1: Introduction

Discussion:

1. Discuss with your class the importance of our dress and appearance.

Section 2: The Modest Dress

عَنْ عَمْرُو بْنِ شُعَيْبٍ عَنْ آبِيهِ
عَنْ جَدِّهِ قَالَ قَالَ رَسُولُ اللهِ صَلَّى
اللهُ عَلَيْهِ وَسَلَّمَ اِلْبَسُوا مَا لَمْ
يُخَالِطْهُ إِسْرَافٌ وَلَا مَخِيلَةٌ ۔

(اَحْمَدُ وَ النَّسَائِيُّ وَابْنُ مَاجَةَ)

Amar ibn Shuayb reports from his father
who reports from his grandfather
that the Messenger of God (ﷺ) said:
Put on any clothes which do not show
extravagance and arrogance.
(Ahmad, Nisai and Ibn Majah)

عَنْ سَمُرَةَ اَنَّ النَّبِيَّ صَلَّى اللهُ
عَلَيْهِ وَسَلَّمَ قَالَ اِلْبَسُوا الثِّيَابَ الْبِيْضَ
فَإِنَّهَا اَطْهَرُ وَ اَطْيَبُ ۔

(اَحْمَدُ وَ التِّرْمِذِيُّ وَالنَّسَائِيُّ وَابْنُ مَاجَةَ)

Samrah narrates that
the Prophet (ﷺ) said:
Wear white clothes
because they make a person look clean and attractive.
(Ahmad, Tirmidi, Nisai and Ibn Majah)

عَنْ اَبِى الدَّرْدَاءِ قَالَ قَالَ
رَسُولُ اللهِ صَلَّى اللهُ عَلَيْهِ وَسَلَّمَ اِنَّ
اَحْسَنَ مَا زُرْتُمُ اللهَ فِىْ قُبُوْرِكُمْ
وَمَسَاجِدِكُمُ الْبَيَاضُ ۔

(اِبْنُ مَاجَةَ)

It is stated by Abu Darda that
the Messenger of God (ﷺ) said:
Surely the best (dress) in which
you may meet God in
your graves and mosques is white (dress).
(Ibn Majah)

عَنْ اَبِى هُرَيْرَةَ قَالَ لَعَنَ رَسُولُ
اللهِ صَلَّى اللهُ عَلَيْهِ وَسَلَّمَ اَلرَّجُلَ
يَلْبَسُ لِبْسَةَ الْمَرْاَةِ وَالْمَرْاَةَ تَلْبَسُ
لِبْسَةَ الرَّجُلِ ۔

(اَبُوْدَاؤُدَ)

Abu Hurayra reports that
the Messenger of God (ﷺ)
cursed the man who wore female clothes
and the woman who wore the male dress.
(Abu Daud)

Let's find out what you have learned from

Section 2: The Modest Dress

Discussion:

1. Hold a discussion about why the Prophet told us not to wear clothes which show extravagance or arrogance.

2. White clothes have been recommended in two Traditions here. Discuss this.

3. Discuss the importance of why the Prophet curses men who wear female clothes and women who wear men's clothes.

Section 3: Our Form and Appearance

عَنِ ابْنِ عُمَرَ قَالَ قَالَ رَسُوْلُ
اللهِ صَلَّى اللهُ عَلَيْهِ وَسَلَّمَ مَنْ تَشَبَّهَ
بِقَوْمٍ فَهُوَ مِنْهُمْ ۔

(اَحْمَدُ وَاَبُوْدَاؤُدَ)

Ibn Umar states that
the Messenger of God (ﷺ) said:
Whoever imitates a people
is among them.
(Ahmad and Abu Daud)

عَنِ ابْنِ عَبَّاسٍ قَالَ قَالَ النَّبِيُّ
صَلَّى اللهُ عَلَيْهِ وَسَلَّمَ لَعَنَ اللهُ
الْمُتَشَبِّهِيْنَ مِنَ الرِّجَالِ بِالنِّسَاءِ
وَالْمُتَشَبِّهَاتِ مِنَ النِّسَاءِ بِالرِّجَالِ

(الْبُخَارِيُّ)

Ibn Abbas reports that
the Prophet (ﷺ) said:
God's curse befalls those men
who imitate women
and those women who imitate men.
(Bukhari)

عَنْ اَبِي هُرَيْرَةَ اَنَّ رَسُوْلَ اللهِ
صَلَّى اللهُ عَلَيْهِ وَسَلَّمَ قَالَ مَنْ كَانَ
لَهُ شَعْرٌ فَلْيُكْرِمْهُ

(اَبُوْدَاوُدَ)

Abu Hurayra narrates that
the Messenger of God (ﷺ) said:
Whoso has hair, let him look after it.
(Abu Daud)

عَنْ عَلِيٍّ قَالَ نَهَى رَسُوْلُ اللهِ
صَلَّى اللهُ عَلَيْهِ وَسَلَّمَ اَنْ تَحْلِقَ
الْمَرْأَةُ رَاسَهَا ۔

(النَّسَائِيُّ)

Ali states that
the Messenger of God (ﷺ)
prohibited women from shaving the hair (of their head).
(Nisai)

Let's find out what you have learned from

Section 3: Our Form and Appearance

Discussion:

1. Discuss with your class the various points made in this section.

Section Answers:

Section 1: Introduction

1. Answers vary.

Section 2: The Modest Dress

1. Answers vary.
2. Answers vary.
3. Answers vary.

Section 3: Our Form and Appearance

1. Answers vary.

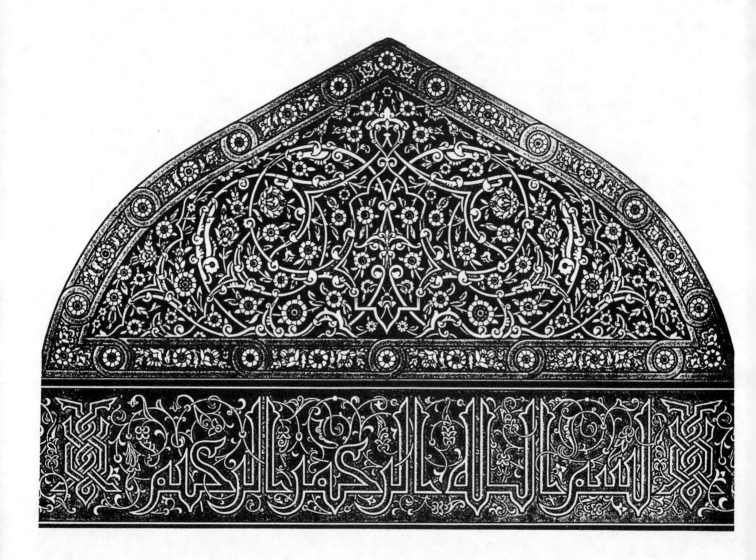

9
Good Character and Conduct

Section 1: Introduction

Good character and conduct are keys to pleasant and successful living. Most of our troubles and failures are due to a lack of character. Healthy morals enable a child to face all problems of life quite confidently. What are good character and conduct? What are excellent morals? This chapter offers those simple Traditions which throw light on various aspects of morality. The discussion is divided into the following four sections:

Section 2: The Importance of a Sound Character

Good character and conduct have high value in the Muslim way of life. The Prophet said that all people of the world were "God's family." He himself did good to everyone and advised everyone to do good to others.

Section 3: Goodwill and Open Mind

A Muslim must always have all the good intentions and goodwill for everyone. A good child approaches people and situations with an open mind and a large heart.

Section 4: Sweet Words and Deeds

Sweet words have a magical effect. But should the matter end with the words alone? No, not all. What, after all, is the use of saying good words to others when we do not mean them? All sweet words must be accompanied by sweet deeds.

Section 5: Prudence and Moderation

Another sign of good character is wisdom and prudence in all fields of life. Similarly, balance and moderation in daily dealings are also a proof of sound character.

These charming sayings of the Prophet play a great role in character development. Their purpose is to help you grow into useful citizens. You will take pleasure in doing good to everyone around you.

Let's find out what you have learned from
Section 1: Introduction

Discussion:

1. Discuss good character and conduct according to the sections in this chapter.

Section 2: The Importance of a Sound Character

عَنْ أَنَسٍ وَعَنْ عَبْدِ اللهِ قَالَ
قَالَ رَسُوْلُ اللهِ صَلَّى اللهُ عَلَيْهِ وَسَلَّمَ
اَلْخَلْقُ عِيَالُ اللهِ فَأَحَبُّ الْخَلْقِ
اِلَى اللهِ مَنْ أَحْسَنَ اِلَى عِيَالِهِ ۔

(اَلْبَيْهَقِيُّ)

It is reported by Anas and Abd Allah that
the Messenger of God (ﷺ) said:
People are God's family.
Therefore, the dearest to God
is the person who is kind to his (or her) family.
(Bayhaqi)

عَنْ رَجُلٍ مِنْ مُزَيْنَةَ قَالَ
قَالُوْا يَا رَسُوْلَ اللهِ مَا خَيْرُ مَا أُعْطِىَ
الْاِنْسَانُ قَالَ الْخُلُقُ الْحَسَنُ ۔

(اَلْبَيْهَقِيُّ)

It is reported by a man
from the Muzayna tribe that people asked:
O Messenger of God! What is the best of
what the human being has been given?
He replied: Good conduct.
(Bayhaqi)

عَنْ عَبْدِ اللّٰهِ بْنِ عَمْرٍ وَقَالَ قَالَ
رَسُولُ اللّٰهِ صَلَّى اللّٰهُ عَلَيْهِ وَسَلَّمَ إِنَّ
مِنْ خِيَارِكُمْ أَحْسَنَكُمْ أَخْلَاقاً ۔

(مُتَّفَقٌ عَلَيْهِ)

Abd Allah ibn Amr reported that
the Prophet (ﷺ) said:
Certainly the best of you are those
who have excellent morals.
(Agreed upon)

عَنْ أَبِى هُرَيْرَةَ قَالَ قَالَ
رَسُولُ اللّٰهِ صَلَّى اللّٰهُ عَلَيْهِ وَسَلَّمَ أَكْمَلُ
الْمُؤْمِنِينَ إِيمَاناً أَحْسَنُهُمْ خُلُقاً ۔

(رَأَبُوْدَاوُدَ وَالدَّارِمِيِّ)

Abu Hurayra narrated that
the Messenger of God (ﷺ) said:
The best amongst the believers in faith
are the best among them in character.
(Abu Daud and Darimi)

عَنْ عَبْدِ اللهِ بِنِ عَمْرٍو قَالَ
قَالَ رَسُولُ اللهِ صَلَّى اللهُ عَلَيْهِ وَسَلَّمَ
اِنَّ مِنْ اَحَبِّكُمْ اِلَيَّ اَحْسَنَكُمْ
اَخْلَاقًا
(الْبُخَارِيُّ)

**Abd Allah ibn Amr reported that
the Messenger of God (ﷺ) said:
The dearest to me among you is
the best of you in conduct.
(Bukhari)**

عَنْ اَبِي ثَعْلَبَةَ الْخُشَنِيِّ اَنَّ
رَسُولَ اللهِ صَلَّى اللهُ عَلَيْهِ وَسَلَّمَ قَالَ
اِنَّ اَحَبَّكُمْ اِلَيَّ وَاَقْرَبَكُمْ مِنِّي
يَوْمَ الْقِيٰمَةِ اَحَاسِنُكُمْ اَخْلَاقًا۔
(الْبَيْهَقِيُّ)

**Abu Thalbah al-Khushini states that
the Messenger of God (ﷺ) said:
The dearest and the nearest to me
among you on the Day of Resurrection
shall be the best of you in morals.
(Bayhaqi)**

Let's find out what you have learned from

Section 2: Importance of a Sound Character

Identification:

1. What are the four important characteristics of a sound character?

Discussion:

2. Notice in the Tradition at the bottom of page 82 that the Prophet said the best thing given to us is good conduct. Discuss this with your class.

Section 3: Goodwill and Open Mind

عَنْ عُمَرَ بْنِ الْخَطَّابِ رَضِیَ اللهُ
عَنْهُ قَالَ قَالَ رَسُولُ اللهِ صَلَّی اللهُ عَلَیْهِ
وَسَلَّمَ اِنَّمَا الْاَعْمَالُ بِالنِّیَّاتِ ۔

(مُتَّفَقٌ عَلَیْهِ)

It is reported by Umar ibn al-Khattab that
the Messenger of God (ﷺ) said:
Surely acts depend upon intentions.
(Agreed upon)

عَنْ اَبِیْ هُرَیْرَةَ قَالَ قَالَ رَسُولُ
اللهِ صَلَّی اللهُ عَلَیْهِ وَسَلَّمَ اَلْغِنٰی
غِنَی النَّفْسِ ۔

(مُتَّفَقٌ عَلَیْهِ)

Abu Hurayra states that
the Messenger of God (ﷺ) said:
Richness is the richness
of the self (i.e. self-contentment).
(Agreed upon)

عَنْ اَبِى هُرَيْرَةَ قَالَ قَالَ رَسُوْلُ
اللّٰهِ صَلَّى اللّٰهُ عَلَيْهِ وَسَلَّمَ اِنَّ اللّٰهَ
لَا يَنْظُرُ اِلٰى صُوَرِكُمْ وَ اَمْوَالِكُمْ وَلٰكِنْ
يَنْظُرُ اِلٰى قُلُوْبِكُمْ وَ اَعْمَالِكُمْ.

﴿مُسْلِمٌ﴾

It is narrated by Abu Hurayra that
the Prophet (ﷺ) said:
Surely God does not consider
your figures and wealth.
He rather values your hearts and acts.
(Muslim)

Let's find out what you have learned from

Section 3: Goodwill and Open Mind

Clarification:

1. What does God value most according to the Tradition on page 87?
2. What do our acts depend upon?
3. What do good intentions, self-contentment and acting through our hearts lead to?

Section 4: Sweet Words and Deeds

عَنِ ابْنِ عُمَرَ قَالَ قَالَ رَسُولُ
اللّٰهِ صَلَّى اللّٰهُ عَلَيْهِ وَسَلَّمَ اِنَّ مِنَ
الْبَيَانِ لَسِحْرًا ۔

(الْبُخَارِيُّ)

**Ibn Umar reports that
the Messenger of God (ﷺ) said:
Surely some speech works like magic
(in that it is very effective).
(Bukhari)**

عَنْ اَنَسٍ قَالَ قَالَ رَسُولُ اللّٰهِ
صَلَّى اللّٰهُ عَلَيْهِ وَسَلَّمَ مَرَرْتُ لَيْلَةً
اَسْرِىَ بِى بِقَوْمٍ تُقْرَضُ شِفَاهُهُمْ
بِمَقَارِيضَ مِنَ النَّارِ ۔ فَقُلْتُ يَا
جِبْرِئِيلُ مَنْ هٰؤُلَاءِ ۔ قَالَ هٰؤُلَاءِ
خُطَبَاءُ اُمَّتِكَ الَّذِينَ يَقُولُونَ مَا
لَا يَفْعَلُونَ ۔

(التِّرْمِذِيُّ)

***It is reported by Anas that
the Prophet (ﷺ) said:
The night I was taken to the heavens,
I passed by people whose lips
were being cut with the scissors of hell fire.
I inquired from Gabriel as to who they were.
He replied that they were the preachers
of my community who used to say things
which they did not act upon.
(Tirmidi)***

Let's find out what you have learned from

Section 4: Sweet Words and Deeds

Discussion:

1. The Prophet tells us that good words can work like magic but that the use of good words alone is not enough. We must act upon them. Discuss this with your class.

Section 5: Prudence and Moderation

عَنْ اَبِى ذَرٍّ قَالَ قَالَ لِى رَسُولُ
اللهِ صَلَّى اللهُ عَلَيْهِ وَسَلَّمَ يَا اَبَاذَرٍّ
لَا عَقْلَ كَالتَّدْبِيرِ ۔

(اَلْبَيْهَقِيُّ)

Abu Dhar narrates that
the Messenger of God (ﷺ) said to him:
O Abu Dharr! There is no wisdom like prudence.
(Bayhaqi)

عَنِ ابْنِ عُمَرَ قَالَ قَالَ رَسُولُ
اللهِ صَلَّى اللهُ عَلَيْهِ وَسَلَّمَ اَلْاِقْتِصَادُ فِى
النَّفَقَةِ نِصْفُ الْمَعِيْشَةِ ۔

(اَلْبَيْهَقِيُّ)

It is reported by Ibn Umar that
the Messenger of God (ﷺ) said:
Moderation in expenditure is half of livelihood.
(Bayhaqi)

Let's find out what you have learned from

Section 5: Prudence and Moderation

Discussion:

1. Discuss these two Traditions—acting with temperance and moderation in our spending—with your class and how important it is to have balance in life.

Section Answers:

Section 1: Introduction

1. Answers vary.

Section 2: Importance of a Sound Character

1. Kindness to family, good conduct, excellent morals and good character.
2. Answers vary.

Section 3: Goodwill and Open Mind

1. Our hearts and acts.
2. Our intentions.
3. Goodwill and an open mind.

Section 4: Sweet Words and Deeds

1. Answers vary.

Section 5: Prudence and Moderation

1. Answers vary.

10
Children and Parents

Section 1: Introduction

In the Muslim way of life, parents occupy their rightful place. Respect for parents and their service is an honor which every son and daughter must enjoy. The Prophet stresses the necessity and utility of reducing distances between parents and children. He suggests ways and means of cementing affectionate ties between the two. The Traditions in this chapter explain various aspects of this important issue under the following three headings:

Section 2: Why serve your mother?

Paradise, it is said, lies underneath our mother's feet. If a child loves and obeys his or her mother, he or she has maximum possible chances to flourish in life. On the other hand, an unfortunate child who does not perform his or her duty to his or her mother, has little chance to grow into a happy and successful citizen.

Section 3: Love Your Mother and Father

The Prophet lay the highest stress on affection and service to our mother but that does not mean that our father is to be ignored. Both parents merit respect and obedience from their children. Even an affectionate look at your father and mother brings you the highest appreciation and reward from God.

Section 4: Rebuking and Disobeying Parents

Disobeying parents has been disapproved in Islam. Similarly, abusing one's own or another's parents is considered extremely undesirable.

The obvious purpose of the Prophet's guidance on these vital issues is to bring parents and children closer to each other. Wherever such a healthy relationship between the two exists, both of them enjoy life.

Let's find out what you have learned from

Section 1: Introduction
Discussion:

1. Discuss the importance of one's mother and one's parents in general.

Section 2: Why serve your mother?

عَنْ مُعَاوِيَةَ بْنِ جَاهِمَةَ اَنَّ
جَاهِمَةَ جَاءَ إِلَى النَّبِيِّ صَلَّى اللّٰهُ
عَلَيْهِ وَسَلَّمَ فَقَالَ يَا رَسُولَ اللّٰهِ اَرَدْتُّ
اَنْ اَغْزُوَ وَقَدْ جِئْتُ اَسْتَشِيرُكَ
فَقَالَ هَلْ لَكَ مِنْ اُمٍّ ۔ قَالَ نَعَمْ
قَالَ فَالْزَمْهَا فَاِنَّ الْجَنَّةَ عِنْدَ
رِجْلِهَا ۔
(اَحْمَدُ وَالنَّسَائِيُّ وَالْبَيْهَقِيُّ)

Muawiyya narrates that Jahima came to the Prophet (ﷺ)
and said: O Messenger of God! I have intended to enlist in the
fighting force and I have come to consult you.
He asked: Do you have a mother? He replied: Yes!
He said: Then stick to her for paradise is beneath her feet.
(Ahmad, Nisai and Bayhaqi)

عَنْ اَبِى الطُّفَيْلِ قَالَ رَاَيْتُ النَّبِيَّ
صَلَّى اللّٰهُ عَلَيْهِ وَسَلَّمَ يَقْسِمُ لَحْمًا
بِالْجِعِرَّانَةِ اِذْ اَقْبَلَتِ امْرَاَةٌ حَتَّى
دَنَتْ اِلَى النَّبِيِّ صَلَّى اللّٰهُ عَلَيْهِ وَسَلَّمَ
فَبَسَطَ لَهَا رِدَاءَهُ فَجَلَسَتْ عَلَيْهِ
فَقُلْتُ مَنْ هِىَ ۔ فَقَالُوا هِىَ اُمُّهُ الَّتِى
اَرْضَعَتْهُ ۔

(اَبُوْدَاؤُدَ)

Abu Tufayl reports that he saw the Prophet (ﷺ)
distributing meat near Jeranah.
A lady appeared moving towards the Prophet (ﷺ).
He then spread his sheet for her.
She sat over it. I inquired:
Who is she?
People said: She is his (foster) mother
who breast-fed him.
(Abu Daud)

Let's find out what you have learned from

Section 2: Why serve your mother?

Discussion:

1. While non-Muslims often accuse Muslims of sending young people to the warfront, this Tradition clearly shows that the Prophet felt a young person's *jihad* was under their mother's feet. Discuss this.

Section 3: Love Your Mother and Father

عَنْ اَبِىْ هُرَيْرَةَ قَالَ قَالَ رَجُلٌ
يَارَسُوْلَ اللهِ مَنْ اَحَقُّ بِحُسْنِ صَحَابَتِىْ
قَالَ اُمَّكَ قَالَ ثُمَّ مَنْ ـ قَالَ
اُمَّكَ ـ قَالَ ثُمَّ مَنْ ـ قَالَ اُمَّكَ
قَالَ ثُمَّ مَنْ ـ قَالَ اَبُوْكَ ـ

(مُتَّفَقٌ عَلَيْهِ)

It is stated by Abu Hurayra that a man asked: O Messenger of
God! Who has the greatest right of good company from me?
He replied: Your mother.
He asked: Who next?
He replied: Your mother.
He asked: Then who next?
He replied: Your mother.
He asked: Who next?
He replied: Your father. (Agreed upon)

عَنْ بَهْزِ بْنِ حَكِيْمٍ عَنْ اَبِيْهِ
عَنْ جَدِّهِ قَالَ قُلْتُ يَا رَسُوْلَ اللهِ مَنْ
اَبَرُّ ـ قَالَ اُمَّكَ ـ قُلْتُ ثُمَّ مَنْ
قَالَ اُمَّكَ ـ قُلْتُ ثُمَّ مَنْ ـ قَالَ
اُمَّكَ ـ قُلْتُ ثُمَّ مَنْ ـ قَالَ اَبَاكَ
ثُمَّ الْاَقْرَبَ فَالْاَقْرَبَ ـ

(اَلتِّرْمِذِىُّ وَ اَبُوْدَاوُدَ)

Bahz ibn Hakim reports from his father who reports from his
grandfather who asked:
O Messenger of God! To whom should I do good?
(The Messenger) replied: To your mother.
He asked: Who next?
(The Messenger) said: Your mother.
He asked: Who next?
(The Messenger) replied: Your mother.
He asked: Who next?
The Messenger replied: Your father, then near relatives and
then the nearer relatives. (Tirmidi and Abu Daud)

عَنْ عَبْدِ اللهِ ابْنِ عَمْرٍو قَالَ

قَالَ رَسُوْلُ اللهِ صَلَّى اللهُ عَلَيْهِ وَسَلَّمَ

رِضَى الرَّبِّ فِىْ رِضَى الْوَالِدِ وَسَخَطُ

الرَّبِّ فِىْ سَخَطِ الْوَالِدِ ۔

﴿التِّرْمِذِىُّ﴾

Abd Allah ibn Amr narrates that the Messenger of God (ﷺ) said:
The pleasure of the Lord is in the pleasure of your father and
the displeasure of the Lord
is in the displeasure of your father. (Tirmidi)

عَنِ ابْنِ عَبَّاسٍ اَنَّ رَسُوْلَ
اللهِ صَلَّى اللهُ عَلَيْهِ وَسَلَّمَ قَالَ مَا
مِنْ وَلَدٍ بَارٍّ يَنْظُرُ اِلَى وَالِدَيْهِ نَظَرَ
رَحْمَتِهِ اِلَّا كَتَبَ اللهُ لَهُ بِكُلِّ نَظْرَةٍ
حَجَّةً مَبْرُوْرَةً ۔

(دالبَيْهَقِيُّ)

*It is reported by Ibn Abbas that the Prophet (ﷺ) said:
Whenever any obedient son looks to his parents with a kind
look, God writes for him (or her) credit equal to one accepted
prescribed pilgrimage for every look. (Bayhaqi)*

عَنِ ابْنِ عُمَرَ قَالَ رَسُوْلُ
اللهِ صَلَّى اللهُ عَلَيْهِ وَسَلَّمَ اِنَّ مِنْ
اَبَرِّ الْبِرِّ صِلَةُ الرَّجُلِ اَهْلَ وُدِّ
اَبِيْهِ بَعْدَ اَنْ يُوَلِّيَ ۔

(مُسْلِمٌ)

*Ibn Umar reports that the Messenger of God (ﷺ) said: The
most excellent virtue is a person's kind treatment of his father's
friends after he has passed away. (Muslim)*

Let's find out what you have learned from

Section 3: Love Your Mother and Father

Discussion:

1. Discuss the love a good Muslim shows towards his or her good mother and father.

Section 4: Rebuking and Disobeying Parents

عَنْ عَبْدِ اللهِ ابْنِ عُمَرَ قَالَ قَالَ
رَسُوْلُ اللهِ صَلَّى اللهُ عَلَيْهِ وَسَلَّمَ مِنَ
الْكَبَائِرِ شَتْمُ الرَّجُلِ وَالِدَيْهِ ـ
قَالُوْا يَا رَسُوْلَ اللهِ وَهَلْ يَشْتِمُ
الرَّجُلُ وَالِدَيْهِ ـ قَالَ نَعَمْ يَسَبُّ
اَبَا الرَّجُلِ فَيَسَبُّ اَبَاهُ وَيَسَبُّ
اُمَّهُ فَيَسَبُّ اُمَّهُ   (مُتَّفَقٌ عَلَيْهِ)

It is stated by Abd Allah ibn Umar that
the Messenger of God (ﷺ) said:
A person's rebuking his (or her) parents
is one of the greatest sins.
People inquired: O Messenger of God!
Can a person chide his (or her) parents?
He replied: Yes,
by abusing another person's father
who abuses his (or her) father (in return) or
by abusing his (or her) mother
and he abuses his (or her) mother
(in return).
(Agreed upon)

عَنْ اَبِىْ بَكْرَةَ قَالَ قَالَ رَسُوْلُ
اللهِ صَلَّى اللهُ عَلَيْهِ وَسَلَّمَ كُلُّ الذُّنُوْبِ
يَغْفِرُ اللهُ تَعَالَى مِنْهَا مَا شَاءَ اِلَّا
عُقُوْقَ الْوَالِدَيْنِ فَاِنَّهُ يُعَجِّلُ
لِصَاحِبِهِ فِىْ حَيَاةٍ قَبْلَ الْمَمَاتِ ـ
(الْبَيْهَقِىُّ)

**Abu Bakr reports that
the Prophet (ﷺ) said:
God Almighty may pardon all sins
as He pleases except disobedience to parents.
He rather hastens (to punish) its doer
in his (or her) life before death.
(Bayhaqi)**

عَنْ عَبْدِ اللهِ ابْنِ عَمْرِو قَالَ
قَالَ رَسُوْلُ اللهِ صَلَّى اللهُ عَلَيْهِ وَسَلَّمَ
لَا يَدْخُلُ الْجَنَّةَ مَنَّانٌ وَلَا عَاقٌ وَ
لَا مُدْمِنُ خَمْرٍ ۔

(النَّسَائِيُّ وَالدَّارِمِيُّ)

**It is narrated by Ibn Amr that
the Messenger of God (ﷺ) said:
The boaster of good, the disobedient and the dead-drunk
will not enter paradise.
(Nisai and Darimi)**

Let's find out what you have learned from

Section 4: Rebuking and Disobeying Parents

Discussion:

1. The Traditions emphasize the importance of children obeying their parents because they assume that their parents are good parents who only want the best for their children. Discuss this with your class.

Section Answers:

Section 1: Introduction

1. Answers vary.

Section 2: Why serve your mother?

1. Answers vary.

Section 3: Love Your Mother and Father

1. Answers vary.

Section 4: Rebuking and Disobeying Parents

1. Answers vary.

11
Relations and Attitudes

Section 1: Introduction

What should be your attitude towards people in and outside your home? How should you treat your brothers, sisters, relatives, friends, neighbors and others? A good child must develop the most healthy attitudes towards all people in his or her environment. Prophet Muhammad's Traditions are a source of inspiring guidance. This chapter explains the above issues under the following two headings:

Section 2: Brothers, Sisters and Relatives

How are you to approach your brothers and sisters who may be younger or older than you in age and wisdom? The Prophet recommends love and affection, tolerance and understanding on both sides. He disapproves boycotting people or disregarding human ties.

Section 3: Friends and Neighbors

Friendship is highly valued in Islam. Good friends are necessary for a balanced growth of personality and character. We must have cordial relations with the neighbors also. Neglecting poor neighbors or causing inconvenience to any neighbor is opposed to the Islamic way of life.

The purpose of these Traditions is to make people understand each other. To live healthily and to let mothers live healthily is the central idea of Islam. Practice these pleasant and useful principles. You will then discover a constructive change in your thought and behavior.

Let's find out what you have learned from

Section 1: Introduction

Discussion:

1. Discuss how your relations are towards others.

Section 2: Brothers, Sisters and Relatives

عَنْ سَعِيْدِ ابْنِ الْعَاصِ قَالَ قَالَ
رَسُوْلُ اللهِ صَلَّى اللهُ عَلَيْهِ وَسَلَّمَ حَقُّ
كَبِيْرِ الْاِخْوَةِ عَلَى صَغِيْرِهِمْ كَحَقِّ
الْوَالِدِهِ

(الْبَيْهَقِيُّ)

It is reported from Said ibn al-Aas that
the Prophet (ﷺ) said:
The elder brother's right over the younger brother
is like the right of his father.
(Bayhaqi)

عَنْ اَنَسٍ قَالَ قَالَ رَسُوْلُ اللهِ
صَلَّى اللهُ عَلَيْهِ وَسَلَّمَ مَنْ اَحَبَّ اَنْ
يُّبْسَطَ لَهُ فِى رِزْقِهِ وَ يُنْسَأَلَهُ فِى
اَثَرِهِ فَلْيَصِلْ رَحِمَهُ ـ

(مُتَّفَقٌ عَلَيْهِ)

It is narrated by Anas that
the Messenger of God (ﷺ) said:
Whoever wishes that his (or her)
sustenance be made ample for him (or her)
or his (or her) death be delayed,
let him (or her) be kind to his relatives.
(Agreed upon)

عَنْ جُبَيْرِ بْنِ مُطْعِمٍ قَالَ

قَالَ رَسُولُ اللهِ صَلَّى اللهُ عَلَيْهِ وَسَلَّمَ

لَا يَدْخُلُ الْجَنَّةَ قَاطِعٌ ۔

(مُتَّفَقٌ عَلَيْهِ)

Jubayr ibn Mutim reports that
the Messenger of God (ﷺ) said:
One who severs (blood-ties)
shall not enter paradise.
(Agreed upon)

Let's find out what you have learned from

Section 2: Brothers, Sisters and Relatives

Discussion:

1. Discuss your relations with your brothers, sisters and relatives to improve your relations with them.

Section 3: Friends and Neighbors

عَنْ عَبْدِ اللهِ بْنِ عُمَرَ قَالَ قَالَ
رَسُولُ اللهِ صَلَّى اللهُ عَلَيْهِ وَسَلَّمَ خَيْرُ
الْأَصْحَابِ عِنْدَ اللهِ خَيْرُهُمْ لِصَاحِبِهِ ۔

(التِّرْمِذِيُّ وَالدَّارِمِيُّ)

It is narrated by Abd Allah ibn Umar that
the Messenger of God (ﷺ) said:
The best friend in the sight of God
is the best one to his friend.
(Tirmidi and Darimi)

عَنِ ابْنِ عَبَّاسٍ قَالَ سَمِعْتُ
رَسُولَ اللهِ صَلَّى اللهِ عَلَيْهِ وَسَلَّمَ يَقُولُ
لَيْسَ الْمُؤْمِنُ بِالَّذِي يَشْبَعُ وَجَارُهُ
جَائِعٌ إِلَى جَنْبِهِ ۔

(رَوَاهُ الْبَيْهَقِيُّ)

Ibn Abbas reports that he heard
the Messenger of God (ﷺ) saying:
He is not a believer who eats to his full
while his neighbor remains hungry.
(Bayhaqi)

عَنْ اَنَسٍ قَالَ قَالَ رَسُوْلُ اللّٰهِ
صَلَّى اللّٰهُ عَلَيْهِ وَ سَلَّمَ لَا يَدْخُلُ الْجَنَّةَ
مَنْ لَا يَأْمَنْ جَارُهُ بَوَائِقَهُ ۔

(مُسْلِمٌ)

Anas reports that
the Messenger of God (ﷺ) said:
One whose neighbor is not safe from his misdeeds
shall not enter paradise.
(Muslim)

Let's find out what you have learned from

Section 3: Friends and Neighbors

Discussion:

1. Evaluate your relations and attitude towards your friends and neighbors and try to improve them. Discuss ways of doing this.

Section Answers:

Section 1: Introduction

1. Answers vary.

Section 2: Brothers, Sisters and Relatives

1. Answers vary.

Section 3: Friends and Neighbors

1. Answers vary.

12
Brotherhood and Sisterhood

Section 1: Introduction

Love is the basic food for a wholesome life. Islam is the religion of love and affection. The entire world is a brotherhood/sisterhood of God's people. Love and be loved is the wisdom which the Prophet preached and practiced. This chapter presents a few selected Traditions on this important theme. The discussion is divided into two sections is as follows:

Section 2: Islamic Brotherhood/Sisterhood

Muslims all over the world are united into the bonds of affectionate brotherhood/sisterhood. Muslims must develop themselves and help other Muslims develop into decent citizens. What should they do when they find their friend is moving in the wrong direction? Should they go on helping them even when they are committing cruelty, injustice or indecency? No, never! Islamic brotherhood/sisterhood demands that we should always persuade all wrongdoers to behave properly.

Section 2: Love For All People

Is love and affection meant for Muslims alone? Do others also deserve our attention and kindness? Certainly yes. As a matter of fact a Muslim is an ambassador of affection and love, peace and harmony for the entire world. The Prophet made it quite clear that those who do not practice universal love and affection have no place in the brotherhood/sisterhood of Islam.

Needless to say that these Traditions focus on a burning topic of the day. We must all realize that neither an individual nor any nation could make any progress without believing and practicing mutual love and affection sincerely.

Let's find out what you have learned from

Section 1: Introduction

Discussion:

1. Discuss ways of forming brotherhoods and sisterhoods among yourselves.

Section 2: Islamic Brotherhood/Sisterhood

عَنْ اَنَسٍ قَالَ قَالَ رَسُوْلُ اللهِ
صَلَّى اللهُ عَلَيْهِ وَ سَلَّمَ وَالَّذِىْ نَفْسِىْ
بِيَدِهٖ لَا يُؤْمِنُ عَبْدٌ حَتّٰى يُحِبَّ
لِاَخِيْهِ مَا يُحِبُّ لِنَفْسِهٖ

(مُتَّفَقٌ عَلَيْهِ)

It is reported by Anas that
the Messenger of God (ﷺ) said:
By the One Who controls my life,
no one could be a believer unless he (or she)
wishes for his brother (or sister)
what he (or she) wishes for himself (or herself).
(Agreed upon)

عَنْ اَبِىْ هُرَيْرَةَ قَالَ قَالَ
رَسُوْلُ اللهِ صَلَّى اللهُ عَلَيْهِ وَسَلَّمَ اِنَّ
اَحَدَكُمْ مِرْاَةُ اَخِيْهِ ۔

(اَلتِّرْمِذِىُّ)

Abu Hurayra narrates that
the Prophet (ﷺ) said:
Surely each one of you is a mirror
for his (or her) brother (or sister).
(Tirmidi)

عَنْ اَبِىْ هُرَيْرَةَ قَالَ قَالَ
رَسُوْلُ اللهِ صَلَّى اللهُ عَلَيْهِ وَسَلَّمَ
اَلْمُسْلِمُ اَخُ الْمُسْلِمِ لَايَظْلِمُهُ وَ
لَايَخْذُلُهُ وَلَايَحْقِرُهُ ۔

(مُسْلِمٌ)

Abu Hurayra reports that
the Messenger of God (ﷺ) said:
A Muslim is a brother (or sister)
of another Muslim.
He (or she) should not be wronged, insulted or belittled.
(Muslim)

عَنْ اَنَسٍ قَالَ قَالَ رَسُوْلُ اللهِ
صَلَّى اللهُ عَلَيْهِ وَسَلَّمَ اُنْصُرْ اَخَاكَ
ظَالِمًا اَوْ مَظْلُوْمًا ۔ فَقَالَ رَجُلٌ
يَا رَسُوْلَ اللهِ اَنْصُرُهُ مَظْلُوْمًا فَكَيْفَ
اَنْصُرُهُ ظَالِمًا ۔ قَالَ تَمْنَعُهُ مِنَ
الظُّلْمِ فَذَالِكَ نَصْرُكَ اِيَّاهُ ۔

(مُتَّفَقٌ عَلَيْهِ)

Anas states that
the Messenger of God (ﷺ) said:
Help your brother (or sister) whether
he (or she) is an aggressor or grieving.
Then a man asked: O Messenger of God! I can help him (or
her) if he (or she) is grieving but how can I help him (or her)
when he (or she) is an aggressor?
(The Messenger) replied:
Prevent him (or her) from doing wrong.
That, indeed, would be your help to him (or her).
(Agreed upon)

Let's find out what you have learned from

Section 2: Islamic Brotherhood/Sisterhood

Discussion:

1. Discuss ways that we can help each other.

Section 3: Love for All People

عَنْ اَنَسٍ وَعَنْ عَبْدِاللهِ قَالَا
قَالَ رَسُوْلُ اللهِ صَلَّى اللهُ عَلَيْهِ وَسَلَّمَ
اَلْخَلْقُ عِيَالُ اللهِ فَاَحَبُّ الْخَلْقِ اِلَى
اللهِ مَنْ اَحْسَنَ عَلَى عِيَالِه -

(اَلْبَيْهَقِيُّ)

It is reported from Anas and Abd Allah that
the Messenger of God (ﷺ) said:
People are God's family.
The dearest to God is the person
who is kind to his (or her) family.
(Bayhaqi)

عَنْ عَبْدِ اللهِ بْنِ عَمْرٍو قَالَ
قَالَ رَسُوْلُ اللهِ صَلَّى اللهُ عَلَيْهِ وَسَلَّمَ
اَلرَّاحِمُوْنَ يَرْحَمُهُمُ الرَّحْمَنُ
اِرْحَمُوْا مَنْ فِى الْاَرْضِ يَرْحَمْكُمْ مَنْ
فِى السَّمَاءِ -
(اَبُوْدَاوُدَ وَ التِّرْمِذِيُّ)

It is narrated by Abd Allah ibn Amr that
the Messenger of God (ﷺ) said:
God is merciful to kind people.
Be kind to those on earth
and the One in the heavens will be kind to you.
(Abu Daud and Tirmidi)

عَنْ جَرِيرِ بْنِ عَبْدِ اللهِ قَالَ
قَالَ رَسُولُ اللهِ صَلَّى اللهُ عَلَيْهِ وَسَلَّمَ
لَا يَرْحَمُ اللهُ مَنْ لَّا يَرْحَمُ النَّاسَ ۔

(مُتَّفَقٌ عَلَيْهِ)

Jarir states that
the Messenger of God (ﷺ) said:
God has no mercy on the one
who is not kind to people.
(Agreed upon)

عَنِ ابْنِ عَبَّاسٍ قَالَ قَالَ
رَسُولُ اللهِ صَلَّى اللهُ عَلَيْهِ وَسَلَّمَ
لَيْسَ مِنَّا مَنْ لَمْ يَرْحَمْ صَغِيرَنَا
وَلَمْ يُوَقِّرْ كَبِيرَنَا ۔

(التِّرْمِذِيَّ)

It is reported by Ibn Abbas that
the Messenger of God (ﷺ) said:
He is not of us who does not show affection
to our young ones nor respect to our elders.
(Tirmidi)

عَنْ اَبِيْ هُرَيْرَةَ قَالَ قَبَّلَ
رَسُوْلُ اللهِ صَلَّى اللهُ عَلَيْهِ وَسَلَّمَ
اَلْحَسَنَ بْنِ عَلِيٍّ وَعِنْدَهُ الْاَقْرَعُ ابْنُ
حَابِسٍ فَقَالَ الْاَقْرَعُ اِنَّ لِيْ
عَشَرَةً مِنَ الْوَلَدِ مَاقَبَّلْتُ مِنْهُمْ
اَحَدًا ـ فَنَظَرَ اِلَيْهِ رَسُوْلُ اللهِ صَلَّى
اللهُ عَلَيْهِ وَسَلَّمَ ثُمَّ قَالَ مَنْ لَّا
يَرْحَمْ لَا يُرْحَمُ

(مُتَّفَقٌ عَلَيْهِ)

Abu Hurayra narrates that
the Prophet (ﷺ) kissed Hasan ibn Ali (his grandson)
in the presence of Aqra ibn Habis.
Aqra said: Surely I have ten sons.
I have never kissed any one of them.
The Messenger of God (ﷺ) looked at him and said:
He who is not kind will not be shown mercy.
(Agreed upon)

Let's find out what you have learned from

Section 3: Love for All People

Discussion:

1. Discuss the importance of showing mercy and kindness towards others.

Section Answers:

Section 1: Introduction

1. Answers vary.

Section 2: Islamic Brotherhood/Sisterhood

1. Answers vary.

Section 3: Love for All People

1. Answers vary.

13
Misuse of The Tongue

Section 1: Introduction

Our tongue is a wonderful thing. It is like a double-edged sword. It can be used for good as well as for wrongdoing. How to use the tongue properly? The answer has already been given in the the section on Sweet Words and Deeds. What are the improper uses of the tongue? The Prophet answers this question also for you. He makes you understand how harmful it is to misuse the tongue in any way. This chapter has been divided into the following three sections:

Section 2: Telling Lies and talking Nonsense
Falsehood is the most undesirable and the most dreadful thing in the Muslim way of life. Similarly, talking rubbish is no less an evil. Hurling words hither and thither carelessly does not look nice either.

Section 3: No Cursing, No Taunting
Prophet Muhammad (ﷺ) has sternly forbidden blaming and cursing other people. He has also prohibited taunting and jeering any one. Childhood is the right age to understand the nature of these social evils. We should learn to avoid them in our daily dealings.

Section 4: Avoid Mimicking and Backbiting
Would you like to mock at your friends? What if your friends mimic and imitate you jestingly like a monkey? Surely no sensible child would do that. Similarly, backbiting is not a good habit either.

The object of this chapter on this important topic is to emphasize the harms and dangers of the misuse of language. Life becomes far more pleasant and far more successful if the tongue is kept under proper control. Now let us see how the Prophet guides us about the tongue and the words.

Let's find out what you have learned from

Section 1: Introduction
Discussion:

1. Discuss the miseries of one's tongue.

Section 2: Telling Lies and Talking Nonsense

عَنْ سُفْيَانَ بْنِ عَبْدِ اللهِ الثَّقَفِيْ
قَالَ قُلْتُ يَا رَسُوْلَ اللهِ مَا اَخْوَنُ مَا
تَخَافُ عَلَيَّ قَالَ فَاَخَذَ
بِلِسَانِ نَفْسِهِ وَقَالَ هٰذَا۔

(التِّرْمِذِيُّ)

Sufyan ibn Abd Allah al-Saqfy reports that
he inquired: O Messenger of God! What is the most dreadful of
the things which you consider fearful for me?
He states that he caught hold of his tongue and said:
This.
(Tirmidi)

عَنْ اَنَسٍ قَالَ قَالَ رَسُوْلُ اللهِ
صَلَّى اللهُ عَلَيْهِ وَسَلَّمَ مَنْ تَرَكَ
الْكَذِبَ وَهُوَ بَاطِلٌ بُنِيَ لَهٗ
فِيْ رَبَضِ الْجَنَّةِ۔

(التِّرْمِذِيُّ)

Anas narrates that
the Messenger of God (ﷺ) said:
Whoever gives up telling baseless lies,
a house is built for him (or her) by the side of paradise.
(Tirmidi)

عَنْ سُفْيَانَ بْنِ أُسَيْدٍ الْحَضْرَمِيُّ
قَالَ سَمِعْتُ رَسُولَ اللهِ صَلَّى اللهُ عَلَيْهِ
وَسَلَّمَ يَقُولُ كَبُرَتْ خِيَانَةً أَنْ
تُحَدِّثَ أَخَاكَ حَدِيثًا هُوَ لَكَ بِهِ
مُصَدِّقٌ وَأَنْتَ بِهِ كَاذِبٌ ـ
(أَبُو دَاؤُدَ)

Sufyan ibn Usid al-Hazrami states that
he heard the Messenger of God (ﷺ) say:
It is the height of treachery (breach of trust)
that you report news to your brother (or sister)
which he (or she) believes to be true
while you were lying to him (or her).
(Abu Daud)

عَنْ بَهْزِ بْنِ حَكِيمٍ عَنْ أَبِيهِ
عَنْ جَدِّهِ قَالَ قَالَ رَسُولُ اللهِ صَلَّى
اللهُ عَلَيْهِ وَسَلَّمَ وَيْلٌ لِّمَنْ يُحَدِّثُ
فَيَكْذِبُ لِيُضْحِكَ بِهِ الْقَوْمَ ـ وَيْلٌ لَّهُ ـ

(أَحْمَدُ وَالتِّرْمِذِيُّ وَأَبُو دَاؤُدَ وَالدَّارِمِيُّ)

Bahz ibn Hakim reports from his father
who reports from his grandfather
that the Messenger of God (ﷺ) said:
Woe to him who lies
while talking to make people laugh thereby.
Woe to him (or her)!
(Ahmad, Tirmidi, Abu Daud and Darimi)

عَنِ ابْنِ عُمَرَ قَالَ قَالَ رَسُوْلُ
اللهِ صَلَّى اللهُ عَلَيْهِ وَسَلَّمَ اِذَا كَذَبَ
الْعَبْدُ تَبَاعَدَ عَنْهُ الْمَلَكُ مِيْلًا
مِنْ نَتْنِ مَاجَاءَ بِهِ ۔

(التِّرْمِذِيّ)

It is narrated by Ibn Umar that
the Messenger of God (ﷺ) said:
Whenever a person lies,
the angel goes a mile away from him (or her)
on account of the bad smell
of what he (or she) has produced.
(Tirmidi)

Let's find out what you have learned from

Section 2: Telling Lies and Talking Nonsense

Discussion:

1. These Traditions tell us the importance of guarding what we say with our tongue. Discuss this.

Section 3: No Cursing, No Taunting

عَنِ ابْنِ مَسْعُودٍ قَالَ قَالَ
رَسُوْلُ اللهِ صَلَّى اللهُ عَلَيْهِ وَسَلَّمَ
لَيْسَ الْمُؤْمِنُ بِالطَّعَّانِ وَلَا بِاللَّعَّانِ
وَلَا الْفَاحِشِ وَلَا الْبَذِيِّ

(التِّرْمِذِيُّ وَالْبَيْهَقِيُّ)

***Ibn Masud reports that
the Messenger of God (ﷺ) said:
The believer is neither a taunter
nor a curser nor indecent
nor an abuser.
(Tirmidi and Bayhaqi)***

عَنْ أَبِيْ هُرَيْرَةَ أَنَّ رَسُوْلَ اللهِ
صَلَّى اللهُ عَلَيْهِ وَسَلَّمَ قَالَ لَا يَنْبَغِيْ
لِصِدِّيْقٍ أَنْ تَيْكُوْنَ لَعَّانًا

(مُسْلِمٌ)

***It is reported by Abu Hurayra that
the Prophet (ﷺ) said:
It is not proper for a great truthful person
to become a great curser.
(Muslim)***

Section 4: Avoid Mimicking and Backbiting

عَنْ عَائِشَةَ قَالَتْ قَالَ النَّبِيُّ
صَلَّى اللهُ عَلَيْهِ وَسَلَّمَ مَا أُحِبُّ اِنِّي
حَكَيْتُ اَحَدًا وَّاَنَّ لِيْ كَذَا وَكَذَا

(التِّرْمِذِيُّ)

Ayisha reports that
the Messenger of God (ﷺ) said:
I do not like to ape (mimic, copy, imitate)
any one even if this gets me such and such (gains).
(Tirmidi)

عَنْ عَبْدِ الرَّحْمٰنِ بْنِ غَنَمٍ وَ
اَسْمَاءَ بِنْتِ يَزِيدَ اَنَّ النَّبِيَّ صَلَّى اللهُ عَلَيْهِ
وَسَلَّمَ قَالَ شِرَارُ عِبَادِ اللهِ الْمَشَّاؤُنَ
بِالنَّمِيمَةِ الْمُفَرِّقُوْنَ بَيْنَ الْاَحِبَّةِ ۔

(اَحْمَدُ وَالْبَيْهَقِيُّ)

It is reported by Abd al-Rahman ibn Ghanam
and Asma bint Yazid that the Prophet (ﷺ) said:
The worst of God's people
are those who roam about with slander
and those who create separation between friends.
(Ahmad and Bayhaqi)

عَنْ حُذَيْفَةَ قَالَ سَمِعْتُ
رَسُولَ اللهِ صَلَّى اللهُ عَلَيْهِ وَ سَلَّمَ
يَقُولُ لَا يَدْخُلُ الْجَنَّةَ نَمَّامٌ -

(مُسْلِمٌ)

Huzayfah reports that he heard
the Messenger of God (ﷺ) saying:
A backbiter shall not enter paradise.
(Muslim)

Let's find out what you have learned from

Section 4: Avoid Mimicking and Backbiting

Discussion:

1. Describe what a believer is not based on these Traditions.
2. Who does the Prophet say will not enter paradise?

Section Answers:

Section 1: Introduction

1. Answers vary.

Section 2: Telling Lies and Talking Nonsense

1. Answers vary.

Section 3: No Cursing, No Taunting

1. Answers vary.

Section 4: Avoid Mimicking and Backbiting

1. The believer is neither a taunter nor indecent nor an abuser nor a great curser, nor copy and imitate others nor do they slander people nor create separation between friends.
2. A backbiter.

14
Keep Off the Wrong Path

Section 1: Introduction

In the previous chapter we discussed in details the dangers of uncivilized language. The present chapter deals with other varieties of the bad conduct. These evils are easily understandable in the light of Prophet's Traditions. His valuable guidance always helps in keeping off the evil path.

This chapter has been divided into six sections which are as follows:

Section 2: Control Suspicion and Malice

Too much of suspicion about everything is bad. Jealousy and malice are injurious to the growth of personality and character. The Prophet offers practical guidance about the evils and dangers of suspicion and malice.

Section 3: Control Pride and Arrogance

False pride does not pay. Arrogant attitudes are unwise. The Prophet instead advises to adopt humility and mutual understanding.

Section 4: Control Anger and Wrath

Anger is another human weakness. It usually leads to unhappy results for every one. Islam, therefore, recommends self-control and cooling of fiery emotions.

Section 5: Control Ill-will and Dissociation

Why should one have ill-will towards others? Why should a friend desert or dissociate from a friend? The Prophet offers wise guidance in this field as well. He advises humanity to give up all bad feelings and all tensions. He stresses the need for practicing good-will and brotherhood/sisterhood.

Section 6: Avoid Mischief Making

The Prophet's simple words provide a deep understanding of the evil of mischief making. A Muslim has a mission to end all mischief. He must work hard to promote goodness, beauty, justice, peace and harmony throughout the world.

Section 7: Avoid Cruelty and Aggression

To harm any one through words or deeds is simply animal-like. All forms of oppression and aggression are disapproved by the Prophet. Even helping the oppressor in any way has been strictly prohibited in Islam.

The purpose of presenting the Prophet's Traditions on the above mentioned wrongdoings is quite clear. Everyone should understand the nature of these evils in order to be able to avoid them successfully.

Let's find out what you have learned from

Section 1: Introduction

Discussion:

1. Discuss how we stay off the wrong path according to the topics of the Traditions in this chapter.

Section 2: Control Suspicion and Malice

عَنْ اَبِيْ هُرَيْرَةَ قَالَ قَالَ
رَسُوْلُ اللهِ صَلَّى اللهُ عَلَيْهِ وَسَلَّمَ اِيَّاكُمْ
وَالظَّنَّ فَاِنَّ الظَّنَّ اَكْذَبُ الْحَدِيْثِ ۔

(مُتَّفَقٌ عَلَيْهِ)

Abu Hurayra reports that
the Messenger of God (ﷺ) said:
Beware of suspicion
for suspicion is the most false of news.
(Agreed upon)

عَنْ اَبِيْ هُرَيْرَةَ عَنِ النَّبِيِّ صَلَّى
اللهُ عَلَيْهِ وَسَلَّمَ قَالَ اِيَّاكُمْ وَالْحَسَدَ
فَاِنَّ الْحَسَدَ يَاكُلُ الْحَسَنَاتِ كَمَا
تَاكُلُ النَّارُ الْحَطَبَ ۔

(اَبُوْدَاؤُدَ)

Abu Hurayra reports that
the Prophet (ﷺ), said:
Beware of malice
for malice consumes virtues just as fire consumes fuel.
(Abu Daud)

Let's find out what you have learned from

Section 2: Control Suspicion and Malice

Discussion:

1. Discuss what you learned about malice in these Traditions.

Section 3: Control Pride and Arrogance

عَنْ عِيَاضٍ بْنِ حِمَارِ الْمُجَاشِعِيِّ
اَنَّ رَسُوْلَ اللهِ صَلَّى اللهُ عَلَيْهِ وَسَلَّمَ
قَالَ اَنَّ اللهَ اَوْحَى اِلَيَّ اَنْ تَوَاضَعُوْا
حَتّٰى لَا يَفْخَرَ اَحَدًا عَلٰى اَحَدٍ ـ

﴿مُسْلِمٌ﴾

Iyaz ibn Himar al-Mujashi reports that
the Messenger of God (ﷺ) said:
God has (guided) me to the adoption of humility
until no pride over another remains.
(Muslim)

عَنِ ابْنِ مَسْعُوْدٍ قَالَ قَالَ
رَسُوْلُ اللهِ صَلَّى اللهُ عَلَيْهِ وَسَلَّمَ لَا
يَدْخُلُ الْجَنَّةَ مَنْ كَانَ فِىْ قَلْبِهِ
مِثْقَالُ ذَرَّةٍ مِنْ كِبْرٍ ـ فَقَالَ
رَجُلٌ اِنَّ الرَّجُلَ يُحِبُّ اَنْ
يَكُوْنَ ثَوْبُهُ حَسَنًا وَنَعْلُهُ حَسَنًا ـ
قَالَ اِنَّ اللهَ تَعَالٰى جَمِيْلٌ يُحِبُّ
الْجَمَالَ ـ اَلْكِبْرُ بَطَرُ الْحَقِّ وَغَمْطُ
النَّاسِ ـ

﴿مُسْلِمٌ﴾

It is reported by Ibn Masud that
the Messenger of God (ﷺ) said:
Whoso has pride in his heart
even to the weight of an atom shall not enter paradise.
A man then inquired about some one who likes his dress and
shoes to be fine.
He replied: God is beautiful and He loves beauty
but pride is undervaluing the truth and degrading people.
(Muslim)

عَنْ مُعَاوِيَةَ قَالَ قَالَ رَسُولُ

اللهِ صَلَّى اللهُ عَلَيْهِ وَسَلَّمَ مَنْ سَرَّهُ

اَنْ يَّتَمَثَّلَ لَهُ الرِّجَالُ قِيَامًا

فَلْيَتَبَوَّأْ مَقْعَدَهُ مِنَ النَّارِ -

(التِّرْمِذِىُّ وَاَبُوْدَاؤُدَ)

Muawiyya reports that
the Messenger of God (ﷺ) said:
Whoever feels pleased to see people
standing before him
should prepare his (or her) seat in hell fire.
(Tirmidi and Abu Daud)

Let's find out what you have learned from

Section 3: Control Pride and Arrogance

Discussion:

1. What do these Traditions tell us to adopt and from what to turn away.
2. What does the Tradition on the top of page 130 say about beauty?

Section 4: Control Anger and Wrath

عَنْ اَبِىْ هُرَيْرَةَ اَنَّ رَجُلًا
قَالَ لِلنَّبِىِّ صَلَّى اللهُ عَلَيْهِ وَسَلَّمَ
اَوْصِنِىْ قَالَ لَا تَغْضَبْ ـ فَرَدَّ ذٰلِكَ
مِرَارًا قَالَ لَا تَغْضَبْ

(الْبُخَارِىّ)

Abu Hurayra reports that a person
asked the Prophet (ﷺ): Advise me.
He replied: Do not get angry.
The man repeated his question several times, but the Prophet
each time replied: Do not get angry.
(Bukhari)

عَنْ اَبِىْ هُرَيْرَةَ قَالَ قَالَ
رَسُوْلُ اللهِ صَلَّى اللهُ عَلَيْهِ وَسَلَّمَ
لَيْسَ الشَّدِيْدُ بِالصُّرْعَةِ ـ اِنَّمَا الشَّدِيْدُ
الَّذِىْ يَمْلِكُ نَفْسَهُ عِنْدَ الْغَضَبِ ـ

(مُتَّفَقٌ عَلَيْهِ)

Abu Hurayra reports that
the Messenger of God (ﷺ) said:
The strong person is not one
who can wrestle people to the ground
but surely the strong person is one
who can control himself (or herself) at the time of anger."
(Agreed upon)

Let's find out what you have learned from

Section 4: Control Anger and Wrath

Clarification:

1. The strong person.
2. The best advice.

Section 5: Control Ill-will and Dissociation

عَنْ اَبِىْ اَيُّوْبَ الْاَنْصَارِيِّ قَالَ
رَسُوْلُ اللهِ صَلَّى اللهُ عَلَيْهِ وَسَلَّمَ
لَا يَحِلُّ لِلرَّجُلِ اَنْ يَّنْتَهَجَرَ اَخَاهُ
فَوْقَ ثَلثِ لَيَالٍ ۔

(مُتَّفَقٌ عَلَيْهِ)

Abu Ayyub al-Ansari narrates that
the Messenger of God (ﷺ) said:
It is not lawful for any person
to cut off relations with his brother (or sister)
for more than three nights.
(Agreed upon)

عَنْ عَائِشَةَ اَنَّ رَسُوْلَ اللهِ
صَلَّى اللهُ عَلَيْهِ وَسَلَّمَ قَالَ لَا يَكُوْنُ
لِمُسْلِمٍ اَنْ يَهْجُرَ مُسْلِمًا فَوْقَ
ثَلثَةٍ ۔

(اَبُوْدَاؤُدَ)

Ayisha reports that
the Messenger of God (ﷺ) said:
It is not desirable for a Muslim
to sever relations with another Muslim
for more than three days.
(Abu Daud)

عَنْ آبِي هُرَيْرَةَ اَنَّ رَسُوْلَ اللهِ
صَلَّى اللهُ عَلَيْهِ وَسَلَّمَ قَالَ لَا يَحِلُّ
لِمُسْلِمٍ اَنْ يَّهْجُرَ اَخَاهُ فَوْقَ ثَلَثَةٍ
فَمَنْ هَجَرَ فَوْقَ ثَلَثٍ فَمَاتَ
دَخَلَ النَّارَ۔

(اَحْمَدُ وَ اَبُوْدَاؤُدَ)

Abu Hurayra states that
the Messenger of God (ﷺ) said:
It is unbecoming for a Muslim
to desert his brother (or sister)
for over three days.
Whoever remains separated
for more than three (days) and dies,
shall enter hell.
(Ahmad and Abu Daud)

Let's find out what you have learned from

Section 5: Control Ill-will and Dissociation

Discussion:

1. Discuss the importance of good family relations in Islam based on these Traditions.

Section 6: Avoid Mischief Making

عَنْ اَبِى هُرَيْرَةَ عَنِ النَّبِيِّ صَلَّى
اللهُ عَلَيْهِ وَسَلَّمَ قَالَ اِيَّاكُمْ وَسُوْءَ
ذَاتِ الْبَيْنِ فَاِنَّهَا الْحَالِقَةُ

(التِّرْمِذِىّ)

Abu Hurayra reports
the Prophet (ﷺ) said:
Avoid mischief making
against each other
for it is destructive.
(Tirmidi)

عَنْ اَبِى الدَّرْدَاءِ قَالَ قَالَ
رَسُوْلُ اللهِ صَلَّى اللهُ عَلَيْهِ وَسَلَّمَ فَسَادُ
ذَاتِ الْبَيْنِ هِىَ الْحَالِقَةُ

(التِّرْمِذِىُّ وَ اَبُوْدَاوُدَ)

Abu Darda narrates that
the Messenger of God(ﷺ) said:
Causing a rift between two Muslims
is destructive.
(Tirmidi and Abu Daud)

Let's find out what you have learned from

Section 6: Avoid Mischief Making

Discussion:

1. Discuss the importance of holding fast to the rope of Allah and not being divided.

Section 7: Avoid Cruelty and Aggression

عَنْ عِيَاضِ بْنِ حِمَارِ الْمُجَاشِعِيّ
اَنَّ رَسُوْلَ اللهِ صَلَّى اللهُ عَلَيْهِ وَسَلَّمَ
قَالَ اَنَّ اللهَ اَوْحٰى اِلَىَّ اَنْ لَا يَبْغِیْ
اَحَدٌ عَلٰى اَحَدٍ ۔
(مُسْلِمٌ)

Iyaz ibn Himar al-Mujashi reports that
the Messenger of God (ﷺ) said:
God has revealed to me
that no one should oppress any one.
(Muslim)

عَنْ اَوْسِ بْنِ شُرَحْبِيلَ اَنَّهُ
سَمِعَ رَسُوْلَ اللهِ صَلَّى اللهُ عَلَيْهِ وَسَلَّمَ
يَقُوْلُ مَنْ مَشَى مَعَ ظَالِمٍ لِيُقَوِّيَهُ
وَهُوَ يَعْلَمُ اَنَّهُ ظَالِمٌ فَقَدْ خَرَجَ
مِنَ الْاِسْلَامِ ۔

(اَلْبَيْهَقِيُّ)

Aws ibn Shurahbil states that
he heard the Messenger of God (ﷺ) say:
Whoever walks with a tyrant
to strengthen him
and he knows that he is a tyrant
has indeed gone out of Islam.
(Bayhaqi)

Let's find out what you have learned from

Section 7: Avoid Cruelty and Aggression

Discussion:

1. The Traditions are very firm that a Muslim should not be a tyrant or an oppressor. Discuss people you know who should learn these Traditions.

Section Answers:

Section 1: Introduction

1. Answers vary.

Section 2: Control Suspicion and Malice

1. Answers vary.

Section 3: Control Pride and Arrogance

1. Adopt humility and turn away from pride.
2. God is beautiful and loves beauty.

Section 4: Control Anger and Wrath

1. The strong person is one who can control his or her anger.
2. The best advice is not to get angry.

Section 5: Control Ill-will and Dissociation

1. Answers vary.

Section 6: Avoid Mischief Making

1. Answers vary.

Section 7: Avoid Cruelty and Aggression

1. Answers vary.

NOTES

NOTES

NOTES

RECOMMENDED SUPPLEMENTARY BOOKS
FOR ISLAMIC SCHOOLS

A YOUNG MUSLIM'S GUIDE TO THE MODERN WORLD	S. HOSSEIN NASR
A. B. C. ISLAMIC READER	M. A. QAZI
ARABIC ALPHABET COLORING BOOK	K. P.
ARABIC ALPHABET (POSTERS/CARDS)	K. P.
ARABIC ALPHABET NUMBERS (BOTH SIDES), LAMINATED	K. P.
ARABIC WRITING FOR BEGINNERS I, II, III	Z. H. QURESHI
CALIPHS OF ISLAM (SET OF 4 BOOKS)	A. R. SHAD
COLOR AND LEARN MUSLIM NAMES	K. P.
COLOR AND LEARN THE NAMES OF THE FAMILY OF THE PROPHET	K. P.
COLOR AND LEARN THE NAMES OF THE PROPHETS	K. P.
COLOR AND LEARN SALAH (PRAYER)	K. P.
COLOR A STORY OF ADAM	K. P.
COLOR A STORY OF NUH	K. P.
ELEMENTARY TEACHINGS OF ISLAM	A. A. SIDDIQUI
GATEWAY TO ISLAM (SET OF 4 BOOKS)	S. J. DORAY
GUIDING CRESCENT (STORYBOOK)	M. IQBAL
HEROES OF ISLAM (SET OF 12 BOOKS)	M. ASHRAF
HISTORY OF ISLAM, PART I	L. BAKHTIAR
HISTORY OF ISLAM, PART II	L. BAKHTIAR
AMMA (30TH PART): ARABIC, ENGLISH, TRANSLITERATION	K. P.
IMAM (BASIC BELIEFS)	S. A. HASHIM
ISLAMIC ACTIVITY BOOK I, II, III	H. JAMIL
ISLAMIC BOOKS FOR CHILDREN (SET OF 18 BOOKS)	A. S. HASHIM
ISLAMIC ETHICS AND PERSONAL CONDUCT	A. S. HASHIM
LESSONS IN ISLAM (SET OF 5 BOOKS)	M. ASHRAF
MUHAMMAD, THE LAST MESSENGER, SR. LEVEL, I, II	A. ATHAR
MUHAMMAD, THE LAST PROPHET, JR. LEVEL, I, II + WORKBOOK	A. ATHAR
MUHAMMAD'S COMPANIONS I: ESSAYS ON SOME WHO BORE WITNESS	L. BAKHTIAR
NINETY-NINE NAMES OF ALLAH POSTERS (B/W)	K. P.
PROPHETS: MODELS FOR HUMANITY (THEIR BIOGRAPHIES)	A. ATHAR
PRIMER OF ISLAM	K. P.
QURAN FOR CHILDREN	A. RAUF
QURAN MADE EASY (YASSAR-NAL-QURAN)	S. A. BEHLIM
SHORT SURAS FOR PRAYERS	M. A. QAZI
WHAT EVERYONE SHOULD KNOW ABOUT ISLAM AND MUSLIMS	S. HANEEF
ZEENAT'S MOSQUES OF THE WORLD COLORING BOOKS I, II	Z. SHAREEF

NOTES